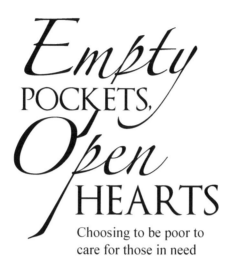

Empty
POCKETS,
Open
HEARTS

Choosing to be poor to
care for those in need

JIM AND DEBBIE STRIETELMEIER

authorHOUSE®

AuthorHouse™
1663 Liberty Drive
Bloomington, IN 47403
www.authorhouse.com
Phone: 1 (800) 839-8640

Published by AuthorHouse 12/29/2016

ISBN: 978-1-5246-5744-4 (sc)
ISBN: 978-1-5246-5743-7 (e)

Print information available on the last page.

Any people depicted in stock imagery provided by Thinkstock are models, and such images are being used for illustrative purposes only. Certain stock imagery © Thinkstock.

This book is printed on acid-free paper.

Because of the dynamic nature of the Internet, any web addresses or links contained in this book may have changed since publication and may no longer be valid. The views expressed in this work are solely those of the author and do not necessarily reflect the views of the publisher, and the publisher hereby disclaims any responsibility for them.

Scripture quotations marked NASB are taken from the *New American Standard Bible®,* Copyright © 1960, 1962, 1963, 1968, 1971, 1972, 1973, 1975, 1977, 1995 by The Lockman Foundation. Used by permission.

Scripture quotations marked KJV are from the Holy Bible, King James Version (Authorized Version). First published in 1611. Quoted from the KJV Classic Reference Bible, Copyright © 1983 by The Zondervan Corporation.

*In honor of Charlie and Lori Nye,
who encouraged us to write.*

Empty Pockets Open Hearts is storytelling about the troubles of ministering to American poverty. It opens biblical passages, with a biblical application.

Empty Pockets open hearts could easily be used for Bible studies, midweek book studies, Sunday Bible study and Bible colleges. It would make a good info textbook for anyone studying Urban Ministry.

The problems of American poverty grow larger. A great gap has divided those who have from those who have not. *Empty Pockets, Open Hearts* embraces the great suffering that come with incarnational ministry to the poor. It also tells you that our God has a plan. That plan is victory and joy for those who lay down their lives in service to God and the people that God calls "the Least of These."

GOD GRANTS VICTORY TO :
Anyone who will first seek
His kingdom and righteousness
Children in need of Education
The hungry
Strangers in the land, or immigrants
Orphans and widows
The Fatherless
The Addicted
Prostitutes
The Oppressed
And all of us trying to help.

Empty Pockets, Open Hearts will help you and your church know where to start. It will tell you about the joy along the way. And it may just tell you where you could end up.

Contents

INTRO

We are Christians who choose to be poor. We love the poor. We identify with the poor. Our church is poor and most of our friends are poor. If we have extra money, we share it with the poor. Debbie says that there is not enough money in the city to keep us from being poor. What she means by that is that when we have extra money it goes to help those around us. Instead of home improvements or retirement accounts, we care for the emergency needs of those in church. All this seems quite normal to those who live here. It is somewhat like being some of the only people with clean water in a desperate country. If we were not to share, we would be considered greedy, thoughtless and mean by the people around us, and the gospel would be limited. We have not made a vow of poverty though. We haven't had to. Where we minister, poverty comes naturally.

People who visit Neighborhood Fellowship seem to have one of two reactions. There are those who are repelled by our acceptance of the problems of poverty in the inner-city—the dirt and grime, simple speech, poor hygiene, poor ways and broken things that come from the grinding nature of need, and there are those who see the same things we see, but like us, envision them as an opportunity for the Gospel. It is often dirty where we live. The buildings, the streets, the sidewalks, even the people sometimes. But dirt is where things grow. Crumbling exteriors and poor hygiene are easily remedied; it's the inside God is concerned with. The broken things are mended by those Isaiah says will be rebuilders of walls. That's us—builders of walls.

Our lives among the poor include the realities of greens and cornbread. On occasion, meat has been a spice in our lives rather than a staple. Some of our friends experience regular homelessness. Many of them are in more need than we are.

We often say that God has given us the abundant life, a life together, where we experience the depths of sorrow as well as the heights of joy. We know the joys of children adopted into the church family when biological mothers are unable to care for them. We know poverty in the valley of want and we know poverty on the hilltop of spiritual reward that is gained by faith.

You might think that we would boast a qualification other than poverty for writing a book. Poverty, however, is the first qualification for true life. Truly living people recognize that they are destitute. Without recognizing this one fact, no one can have a real relationship with God. No one has anything to offer God. Even our good works, done apart from God, only compare to filthy rags. So, truly, we are all poor when it comes to our souls. Yet some are also poor when it comes to their material standing. This group, according to the book of James, is rich in faith. This group has something to say to our more affluent brothers and sisters.

Economic poverty seems to be so much at the forefront in the early church that when Paul went back to Jerusalem to discuss theological issues with the other Apostles, he said in Colossians, "They changed nothing of my gospel, except to remind me to care for the poor, which we were already doing." If the Apostles wanted to remind Paul of this one thing, then we need to be reminded as well.

Defining the poor on a global scale is easy. Poverty in the world is seen in international headlines. But in our hometowns, it can be more difficult to identify the poor. American poverty is a strange animal. You might be able to spot some of the homeless who are poor, but your neighbor who has some means will do everything in his power to avoid you finding out he doesn't have heat for his house. Warm houses, hot water, and other necessities are required for children. Without these necessities your neighbor's children are at risk of being taken by the Department of Child Services. American standards for poverty and the expectations on the poor are different from the rest of the world.

Our standards for measuring poverty at Neighborhood Fellowship are different from how the world measures poverty as well. We begin with matters of the heart, the feelings of powerless that most people living in poverty have. These feelings provide a platform for hopelessness, a feeling that they are unable to change their circumstances.

The poor often don't believe that they have the means to change their situations. When a poor family finds itself in a desperate school system, they simply accept it. Compounding this hopelessness, the poor live in the highest crime rate areas in our cities and have few health care options. Their diets are killing them because of lack of understanding or lack of opportunity. Some work in conditions that expose them to extraordinary risk. Some are unprotected.

The poor are often taken into the foster system. Or they are those who *should* have been. The poor are the fatherless and the widow whose single defense is the generosity of others or the state. The poor are those disabled people who can find help only in someone who considers them family. The poor are often hidden in the shadows of affluence. Resources are all around in this, the wealthiest country on earth. But like the homeless man who is left window shopping, access to resources is often unavailable to the poor.

Those of us who see God's demands on the church to care for the poor are frustrated as we look at American cities. In our cities we have mixed the criminal and foolish elements of society with those who are truly destitute. The places where the more noble poor can afford to live are the same places where those getting out of prison, or those locked in the drug life, can also afford to live. These are the neglected places. The places where crime is managed, but not solved. These are the neighborhoods and parts of town commonly overlooked—until the properties becomes valuable enough to displace those who have survived the troubles.

When any of us attempt to see where genuine need is, the poor are often obscured by those undeserving of help. Many ask for help, but no one should be assisted in their self-destruction. This mixing of the poor and the criminal confuses everyone as to who the poor truly are. It seems to have so confused the American Church that few venture to live with or near the needy.

The book of I Timothy says to "tell those who are rich in this world's goods to be generous and share." The affluent among us are those who enjoy the best America has to offer. They have choices. Those who have ever lived in the best systems, and weren't thrown out, are the affluent. These systems include cities routinely noted as the best places in the country to raise a family, places with the best healthcare systems, the best schools, and the best banks.

Those who buy the best cars are affluent. Those who have access to the best doctors or dentists, or those who go to the best stores and have bought the best chocolates or best perfumes, then yes, they are affluent. There are certainly richer people than those who occasionally indulge, but most Americans live at the pinnacle of human comforts and freedom. In America, it is far easier to find those with access to wealth than the truly poor.

If the church is responsible in any way for those who suffer in poverty, then we believe that the church is wrong when it hoists Christian expectations on a lost world. Yes, Christians are to pray for peace. We are to pray that our Father's will be done on earth as it is in heaven. But until God changes hearts, we must expect that those who do not know God will not act like Him. Just as John the Baptist and the prophets before him spoke warning to the rich and powerful, it is the church's job to be the witness in the world. We are not to be afraid to call unrighteousness sin. We must point out injustice. However, our message is empty if it does not first call the people of God to righteous action. Righteous words are only winsome and powerful if the righteous acts of the saints of God are seen alongside them.

God speaks comfort to all who will attempt to care. The book of Philippians says, "He who began a good work in us will complete it in the day of Christ Jesus." In Romans, the Apostle asks, "Who will deliver me from the body of this death? Thanks be to God, who gives us the victory through our Lord Jesus Christ." God Himself will help us if we let Him, if we take our responsibility seriously to love our neighbor as ourselves.

As I Timothy teaches, those who are rich are commanded to be generous and to share. All Christians are responsible, but those who have access to this world's resources are the best equipped to help. Just as at a scene of an accident, all who see it are morally responsible to do what they can, but if doctors or nurses are among the observers they are more equipped, more responsible. The church must be likewise instructed. All of us must be responsible, to love our neighbor and to share. The dividends of these choices will produce more joy than one could imagine and give life—abundant life.

CHAPTER 1

HOW DID WE GET HERE?

Welcome to the Neighborhood
Poverty as Part of the Plan
Safety First?
Beyond the Topsoil
Competitive

WELCOME TO THE NEIGHBORHOOD

My wife Debbie and I grew up in two different worlds. Her parents had led their family in giving their lives so that rural communities in California and New Mexico could hear the Gospel. They opened closed churches by helping those dying congregations start over with forgiveness and then evangelism. They lived in the mountains, saw the beauty of God's creation as they lifted up their eyes to the hills and found that their help came from the Lord, the Maker of heaven and earth.

My family was a mix of the Joad family from Steinbeck's "The Grapes of Wrath" (without the benefit of traveling), and the Beverly Hillbillies (without the innocence or humor). We were fish out of water, people who lived above their class in an affluent part of the city. Grinding work and impossible schedules were our daily bread. We were joyless as we banded together with my grandmother, parents and uncle. Our eyes rarely lifted above the level of the hogs and crops we raised. The adults divided their labor—first shift, third shift and morning paper routes. School seemed a refuge. Yet others' perception were important to my grandmother. "Good people go to church," she said. We couldn't get to a morning service. The family work prevented that, but we had to go somewhere. Off to Wheeler Mission and their afternoon "church" service.

Debbie and I met as teenagers through Wheeler Mission Ministries. Wheeler primarily ministered to homeless men from their downtown 1920's building, but they also ministered to families who were all but destitute. It had a square chapel, dark wooden seats and large pull-down doors as room dividers that looked like a roll top desk. The organ and piano sat right of the podium. The same woman who had played the organ since the 1920's was there to help me learn how to lead singing for services. Her name was Goldie Frenzel. Ours was the last wedding that she played at.

Wheeler's building was worn with use in those days. It had the smells that homelessness brings. On certain days, families and unattended children came to the mission. I was one of those kids that Wheeler ministered to. My family had come there for church services since I was twelve. Now I was seventeen and serious about the things of God.

Debbie and I were married at the very camp we met at. We married just before her senior year at Moody. We went back to Chicago where we would finish our training. After school, a brief interlude of internships, and a year-long mission trip to South Africa, we returned to Indianapolis, believing we were being called to the inner-city to minister to the poor.

2

We moved into a pocket of poverty on the eastside of downtown. Our house, a ratty old double, with white aluminum siding, would be unprofessionally remodeled for the purpose of starting a church and housing our family. We would work on our home only to find that the doors would be kicked in while we were away so that thieves could search for any tools we might have left. There was daily gunfire in the alley behind the house. Crime was the business of our neighborhood and drugs were the driving force of that economy. Across the street from our house was a school. Its presence, and federal laws about dealing drugs near a school, kept the front of our house safer, although we saw plenty of weapons drawn outside our front door. One of our next-door neighbors went to work but struggled with an addiction to narcotics. On the other side of us, one of the men in that house was a bounty hunter and wore his sidearm even when mowing the yard.

Our neighborhood's racial divide was about forty percent black, forty percent white and twenty percent Latino. All of us were poor by American standards. All the houses in our neighborhood were thirty years since their last roof or paint job. One of our neighbor's houses caught fire and their roof burnt off. They continued to live in their house through the years of repairs, even as we moved into ours in the midst of our remodel. We were covered in drywall dust and they, with their four kids, were covered in soot. We had a common bond in that we were both working on our houses. We had two preschool girls and a baby boy on the way when we first moved in. Safety for family and our community was our regular conversation. We, and our friends, worked hard on our house and did the best job we could. As G.K. Chesterton said, "If it is worth doing it is worth doing badly." And that is just how we worked on our house.

In those days, Jim's parents divorced and we inherited his mother. Jim's grandmother fell and we inherited her as well. We planned, worked, and adapted to our new, difficult and dangerous surroundings. We looked forward to the time we wouldn't clean with a shovel anymore. We could bear it all because we were on a mission.

We already knew the neighborhood because of our connection to Wheeler Mission. This was also a neighborhood that already knew us. We talked to our friends who had all the excuses about why they couldn't go to church.

We were very obvious in the neighborhood as well. People would approach us and ask what we were doing on the street. We were a new oddity. We were great entertainment because we came into the community when no one moved in, but many moved out. Or at least wanted to. Relationship was the currency of our new community. People wanted to know what side of right and wrong we lived on.

For the first two and a half years, the beginnings of Neighborhood Fellowship met in our house. We also continued to meet with the church that had sent us out. They met in the mornings, but Neighborhood Fellowship met in the afternoon. We met in the afternoons to help take away the excuses from our friends. Those who had jobs worked third shifts. Those who did not work were not up in the morning anyway. The Apostle Paul says to be all things to all men that we might win some. We had services and weekly meals in our home. These meals met a nutritional need for some and a relational need for all of us. Deb did most of the cooking in the early days. We went through several stoves until we got an industrial ten-burner, two-oven stove in the house. Dinner was simple: pasta, chicken, salad, ham and bean soup, vegetable beef soup, spaghetti and lots of bread. The entire church ate with us as we rearranged the living room and set up folding tables. The first Sunday there were twenty one.

We couldn't fit sixty in the house the last time we held Easter dinner at our home, so we ate in the garage that day. The large garage was also where we had Sunday school, even though in the winter its only heat was from a wood-burning stove and donated wood. We continued in the house, hot in the summer, with no air conditioning, and cold in the winter because of leaky windows. We met there until fifty or so people wouldn't regularly fit in the house.

We moved the church to a storefront less than a mile away. That storefront met our church's needs for two years until we had outgrown that space and needed something much more significant in size. We had already grown because of or willingness to meet needs. Hospital runs, a food pantry, help in widows' homes, and care for neighborhood children through Sunday school or Vacation Bible School were the normal activities of the church. Outreach was the point of the church. One afternoon we had eighty neighborhood children for one of the Vacation Bible School meetings. We wore our floor and bathroom and doors out. People were responding to the gospel living in their neighborhood. But more people did not equal more money. More people equaled more need, at least at first.

Neighborhood Fellowship was at an awkward size, age, and maturity level. We needed some help. We prayed and God sent friends to help. We knew of a nearby church building that had suffered the ravages of time and water. Parts of the building were built in 1907, the rest in 1928. It was a mess but it was big enough to hold us. The steel window on the educational building had more than ninety broken panes. It was damp and cold from years of water damage. It smelled of mold. Ceilings were collapsed on the floors. The boiler was ancient and pipes would spring a leak every time we turned it on. The bricks were bowing under the twenty seven windows on the west side. The back wall was three stories tall and rippled from the freeze and thaw. Limestone caps had fallen here and there. Yet it was beautiful in our eyes. It was a platform for future ministry.

Yet on Tenth Street, our church building's thoroughfare, the people were even more frightening than our neighbors near our house. These unreached neighbors included those who walked the street professionally. Some were pimps and prostitutes; others were drug dealers handling whatever was possible on the street. These were people we had not been reaching. These were people we could call to righteousness. The building would be a help.

How could we buy it? Everyone in our congregation was poor. There was food for the hungry, but no money for a building. We could go to a bank and be laughed at, or we could pray. We never asked people to step forward. Others outside our ministry stepped in to ask or provide. The money to buy the building flowed in through individual donations. Our suburban friends talked to one another and made a plan to send money monthly so that we could pay the creatively cobbled mortgage. God sent friends who would help negotiate the purchase. Our mortgage terms allowed us to move in and start working. Plaster was raining from all the ceilings, that is, unless it was actually raining. Then the top floor, the middle floor, and the basement were all wet. The basement flooded in heavy rains, yet this building was a platform to build further ministry from. Buildings are just tools for ministry and this one, even though it had seen better days, much better days, was the one that God had planned for us.

POVERTY AS PART OF THE PLAN

Our family's income fits below most of the standards that the government has for poverty. We qualify for health care at the people's' expense. We qualify for food stamps, but we are unwilling to engage with the difficulty of our state's system. We pay little if anything in taxes and if there is a special program to help the poor, we qualify.

A few years ago every window in our house was replaced. All the lead-painted surfaces were covered and eleven brand new interconnected fire alarms were wired in our house. We were thankful. We thanked the workers and every taxpayer we could find. We were and are still surprised at just how much government money is available to help the poor.

When our kids qualified for the free lunch program at the school across the street, we asked if they could just walk the hundred feet across the street and we could handle their meals. We think that we could have found a way to force the school but they had a safety policy and after all it was "already provided for." Those who knew us at school reacted in an odd way when we didn't send the kids for breakfast or, later in the year, to summer care.

We have humbly tried to identify with the poor of our city. The Scripture demands that we associate with the lowly (Romans 12) and the apostle Paul teaches us to "be all things to all men that we might win some" (I Corinthians 9:22). The Lord Himself took on the form of a servant and became obedient even unto death (Philippians 2). And in Jesus' infancy, Mary and Joseph gave an offering of the poor at the temple (Luke 2:24). Today, it shouldn't seem strange that some of God's people would intentionally join the poor and create a platform for ministry.

7

The easiest way our family has identified with the poor has been with a lack of cash. Sometimes this is accomplished by sharing whatever we have with others in need or by receiving only small compensation.

There are those who have misunderstood our Biblical call as an unfortunate circumstance. "They can't do better," or "That is who they are," can be heard in some church entryways when others attempt to explain who we are or what we do. It may be true, but it is unlikely that we will ever know. Our present status seems semi-permanent.

There are those who see poverty as a problem that we are trying to solve. They are sure of our inevitable failure, but continue to give some to our ministry because of our "big hearts." There are those who assume poverty is something that is earned and therefore deserved. They seem to think that "If we are foolish enough to do church planting among the poor, then we deserve the need that comes with it." Whatever the reason for misunderstanding, we have found poverty is one of our greatest assets for ministry.

The most useful way we have found to identify with the needy has been to live among them. We know poverty as one might say "inside out." We know what the extreme heat of summer can do to an already frustrated neighborhood. We know the desperation of families trying to acknowledge holidays or birthdays that it would be more frugal to ignore. We know, by experience, the humiliation that need has associated with it, as well as the simple pleasures of a shared meal. We know; therefore, we can empathize. We need mercy; so we can be merciful.

Entitlements are often the bane of ministry to the poor. We have talked with many friends about the public assistance issues in our community. We have an acquaintance that came to us for food help just after the family got their disability check. We said, "You have money! You just got your check!" She assured us "that money wasn't for food."

Food comes other ways, but not with cash and rarely with work. This regular relief for the poor creates dependence and the worst entitlement attitude one can imagine. We have seen government entitlements destroy work ethics, family structure, and communities. These entitlements often turn people away from dependence on God and His church. They turn industrious folk to compliant folk who are characterized by dependence rather than skill. No one needs to change their behavior or their belief system when their basic needs are minimally met. Yet the church has not fought for its place in society. Individual Christians too rarely love their neighbors as themselves. Since the government is where to go for tangible help, the church has become irrelevant to the needy.

In our early years of family life, we realized that we qualified for a particular food program. We talked to several friends about it. Some thought it natural that we sign up. Free stuff is good stuff, right? In their minds, it was the same as public education for all children. Others thought it shameful. We consulted with older church leaders and one of them, a farmer, said, "Sometimes they pay me not to plant." Another said, "I vote against it, but accept the system as it is."

We signed up. It wasn't too long before we thought the help was not worth the cost to our dignity. Some programs have helped us. Some have insulted us. All these gifts from our magnanimous government have come with intrusion, as we think they should, but some come with humiliation. All this has been done while we have pursued God and worked at ministry. These financial difficulties have been part of our church life and help us know how others live.

We would rather the help that has come from our government had come from Christians instead. We have invited many financially stable Christians to join with us in using their resources or skills to help others. Some have jumped in with both feet. Most don't know where to begin. There is a stream of help from the people of God. But they first need to be first coaxed into a river, and then a raging torrent. Until the church gets it right or Jesus returns, we struggle with identifying with the poor. To what extent we should identify has been a regular question in our family's heart. We occasionally get worn down by the constant need of our friends and neighbors. We dislike the awkwardness of dealing with government workers, let alone Christian friends on the outside of our poor circle, who just don't agree.

We read the Scriptures and are convinced that someone must not only care for the needy, someone must identify with them and speak on their behalf. What wears us down is not the lack. What wears us down the most is our standing in society. Those who have little seem to have little voice and even less credibility. To be heard, the poor resort to shouting or rioting. We, as part of the poor, are numbered with the criminal and foolish no matter how noble the cause that has brought us to this place of need. Worth is most commonly measured by wealth. Even the church in our country, those who read the same Bible we read, doesn't know that God is paying attention to how we handle the least of these in our communities.

Yet we see the great benefits associated with need. We have gained much more than we have lost. These gifts from God are dearer to our hearts then the comforts we could buy. The fact that God has chosen the poor of this world to be rich in faith is not lost on us. The Lord has honored the very faith that He has given us by doing abundantly more than we have asked or thought. Yet, as Americans, we are tempted from time to time to abandon the problems of the needy and move to more prosperous circumstances. Not that we have figured out comfort, but when we are particularly frustrated we talk about goat farming in some western state. If you have a difficult goat, you might think about eating him.

It seems that the church might be waiting to find the thankful poor in order to help those individuals. It is a joy to see people appreciate the help that we give them. Unfortunately, many give to organizations where thankfulness is lost in the paperwork. We, ourselves, have been part of those ministries.

If you want to see the work of God, we suggest that you get a front row seat. You can spend your time where the poor are. Or it can be done through the humility of getting to know the people you are giving to. As you do, you will find those trained in unthankfulness by their own sinful hearts and our government's entitlements. Did we mention they are called entitlements? Those people will frustrate you even as they do us. But you will also find those who are rich in faith and have been taught by God to be thankful—the very ones that it is a pleasure to help.

SAFETY FIRST

Signs went up in front of our local schools, "Have a safe break." It is our culture's reminder that there are limits to our earthly lives. Accidents are preventable, life can be sustained, tragedy avoided, and people can enjoy the peace that safety brings.

This emphasis on safety not only provides for good things like safer cars, warnings for fire, weather, or carbon monoxide, but it has measurable results. Our state celebrates the decline of "on-the-job deaths." Our nation even keeps record of how safe flight is. Flight, still an amazing thought, is our safest means of travel. Yet safety that is emphasized everywhere, is also the basis of many lawsuits and malpractice claims.

Safety has added strength to our weakness, but it has also driven us away from neighbors who needed us most of all. The concern for safety keeps many of us from the inner-cities where our help is needed. Even in training for emergencies, natural or manmade, we are told to first evaluate the situation for safety. This is wise advice that will prevent piling needless loss upon tragedy. It may, however, become our highest goal when others who might be rescued are at risk.

The last time we took CPR training we were reminded that rescue breathing was no longer required as part of emergency care. It seemed clear that it was for our safety. We have also noticed that many a stranded motorist has remained on the side of the road until professional help could come because it is not "safe" for others to stop.

When neighbors are in need, shouldn't those who are right in our paths be the first to enjoy our Christian kindness? Yet they are often left to themselves because safety has infiltrated the church as one of its highest goals. Safety is a cultural value that must be superseded by God's highest value, love.

"Don't cross into that neighborhood after dark," is a parent's wise advice.

"The problems of the city are someone else's problems."

"We can't invite someone into our home."

"There is nothing you could do for a problem so big."

These are the thoughts of many as they consider their family's physical safety when dealing with the broken places and broken people. We are a nation that has absolved individuals of responsibility for social decay. We wait for the professional, or the politician, to set things right.

In the meantime, our cultural obsession with safety grows.

Our nation's current emphasis is on safe playgrounds. It seems that the lower, safer playgrounds placed at most schools and parks don't provide enough risk or excitement for older kids to disengage from electronics and gain mental health skills for living. Our kids don't learn to master heights or dangerous activities, leaving them harmed in greater ways than mere broken bones. More and more, our nation's kids are anxiety free in the cyber world and in need of medication in the physical world. It seems that safety itself is unsafe.

One of the specific areas where safety has not played out well has been in our city and its school system. When we were children, a federal judge ordered Indianapolis Public Schools to begin bussing in order to integrate the schools. Many friends' families moved outside the school district because "it was not safe."

People moved because of their commitment to neighborhood schools. Others moved because of their independence, but for many it was a cover for classism, racism and the American desire for individual betterment. This drive toward something better, even at the cost of the community, has helped destroy the very thing that made us "safe," secure in community. People moved because it was not "safe." In the end, the once-loved city showed signs of abandonment and decay. The self-fulfilling prophecy was fulfilled; the city became unsafe.

But the isolation of many in the suburbs brought with it a particular lack of social safety. Independence always does. Community was not so easily built elsewhere and in the end, "physical safety" cost us the safety that comes from neighbors who support our families and beliefs. Everyone doesn't know everyone's business anymore. Most families were more on their own and therefore at greater risk of their beliefs and traditions being undermined by large cultural changes seen in public schools and the media. Pursuing physical safety might have secured our physical lives and lost us our communal souls. At the very least, it has upset the personal peace that came from living among those who were watching out for us.

Personal peace and affluence have always been driving forces for immigrants and their children. Ours, however, is a nation of immigrants who wanted freedom first of all. Peace, affluence, and other blessings from God would come with hard work and in God's time. Safety, though desired, was not the immigrants' mantra. Those who have left all to cross borders and begin a new life know that safety comes later. It seems that many have forgotten their biological family's sojourner past. Many immigrants came for religious freedom, freedom to express the Love of God as they saw fit. These traditions and societal beliefs were the foundation for these families and their communities. They would never have exchanged them for something as common as safety.

It seems that many Christians also have forgotten their roots. Many forget that our spiritual family is an assembly of aliens in the world, waiting for a city whose architect and builder is God (Hebrews 11). Safety comes later for us, too. For now, those who are driven by our first priority, love, must risk ourselves for our neighbors.

Those who risk themselves for others are the peacemakers mentioned in the Sermon on the Mount. They shall be called the sons of God because they act like God. They give their lives for the sake of others. We are all called to this high calling. But it is those who understand their spiritual position that are able to put personal safety into its appropriate secondary place. Often they find themselves in unsafe situations ministering to the hungry, the naked, the stranger in the land, not turning away from their own flesh and blood (Isaiah 58). Many find themselves looking to previously abandoned neighborhoods and asking, "What can I do?" And then they do it. They are people who risk for the Gospel. They are wise as serpents and gentle as doves, offering their lives as spiritual sacrifices to God, losing their lives for the Lord's sake. They are the ones who count safety as something that comes only in the presence of God.

BEYOND THE TOPSOIL

From time to time, we look for someone to blame for the destructive problems of the poor in the inner-city. When we are feeling lazy, we blame the government. On really bad days we blame the poor themselves and call them lazy. If it were simply the poor themselves, we would be justified in letting them lie in the beds they have made. If the church is to blame we cannot turn back time, so we need a revival. If someone or something else is to blame, they should be involved in the restoration process. Whoever is at fault has left others to meet the needs of the needy. They left a big mess and it seems that the mess is getting more complicated.

We were contacted a few years ago by a landowner who wanted to give away an entire city block. It was less than two miles from our home. We were impressed with the things that could be done on the land and with the building. We were smitten. We are hopeful dreamers.

This property is on a trail linking the city with its more affluent northern suburbs. We could imagine a future where this land would be of great value and desirable for condos.

We also realized that if the church never gets to jobs and job training, it isn't addressing some of the perpetual needs of the poor. This property could have potential along those lines. We sought every relationship we could think of to help us think through the implications of job training, housing, and retail.

It was perfect with the one exception. The building had been used for more than seventy years as an electroplating factory. It was surrounded by factories that had also contaminated the land. The heavy metals in the ground had polluted the area to such an extent that neighboring properties had to have a foot of topsoil removed and burned before they could be used. Our pledged property was even worse and, because of the costs that cleanup would bring, we had to walk away. Today that land is still polluted and jobs have had to come through other means.

The problems of poverty are mirrored in that foot of topsoil that was contaminated and needed excavating. But when we only concern ourselves with the top foot of contamination, we only deal with the surface issues, not the root causes of the contamination.

Often the mess of poverty is complicated because of the assumptions people make about poverty based only on that top foot of contaminated soil they see. One of the worst assumptions is that all poverty is the same. "Poor folk have poor ways," is one proverb we can do without. We can do without it because it is only half-true. We could just as easily say that "poor people come from poor parents." And that would be just as half-true.

The view that poverty is earned is the same as believing that some piece of land deserved to be polluted. It's like believing that middle-class status is only earned.

A portion of that is true, but it isn't the whole picture. Blaming the victim when extended family or a caring society could have, or should have, stepped in, only makes things worse. We victimize the victim. Self-inflicted poverty is generally the poverty thought of when the subject is discussed; a one-size-fits-all approach to the larger problem is inadequate.

Rarely is there room for poverty to be embraced, used and benefited from. Let me explain. The *problems* in poverty do indeed create suffering, but all suffering is not without purpose. Christ's suffering was just this kind. He asked the Father that if it could pass that it would, but it could not and his suffering was the means to our salvation. The apostle Paul tells us that we are to embrace suffering as part of knowing God. Somehow what seems senseless to us, is part of God's work in us and in the world. Suffering is a means to our growth in godliness. It is often a means for God to walk with His people.

I have never met a kid with braces who didn't think that they included suffering. Yet parents willingly inflict their children with the pain of teeth being adjusted for the pleasure and benefit that momentary discomfort will bring in the future. Yet when we consider suffering in poverty, we often overlook that God, like a parent, may be working in our suffering for our future good.

If we act like the world, our answer is to prevent suffering, to protect ourselves from it and cushion ourselves from it. If we act in faith, we must ask if God is behind the situation.

Should we really answer every need, alleviate every pain? If so, how? With a check? That is the best way to give a disabled person a criminal friend. Free money is a bane. It destroys the industry of the weak and separates individuals from the safety and purpose once found in family. Poverty that leads to godliness must be embraced. Rarely is the root of poverty cured by the most obvious answer, money.

The children of the Great Depression were proud of the lessons they learned in times of economic want. They would have avoided the troubles if they could have, but when faced with them, they adapted and character was formed. They came out of that economic turmoil to later be known as the Greatest Generation. They are the ones who sacrificed for God, country, and neighbor. They helped set the course of the world toward freedom. They are the generation who boasted that they didn't know they were poor until someone told them. They are also the ones who warmly remember the camaraderie of neighbors who knew how to work and share in time of want and need.

Recently, we have come through the Great Recession. All around, people have learned dependence on government and independence from God. Lack of resources within a God-fearing community once helped to build character. Now people have had the destructive lessons of poverty solidified, reinforced with dependence. We have called that help an entitlement. It is something our society demands. It doesn't build virtue because it is owed. It doesn't build gratefulness because it is owed. Something owed is my right, not my responsibility.

Poverty that fails to build character also becomes more prevalent as family values reflect an American independence that teaches and encourages individuals to chase their personal American dream. It means that on too many occasions, I am not my brother's keeper. It means that the village isn't available to help raise a child. This social poverty has torn at the very heart of what it is to be a Christian in America. This is the true generational poverty that spits in the face of Biblical

Christianity. It prevents us from loving God and our neighbor as ourselves. It guarantees learned poverty. It is a lack of care in relationship that prevents us from making good decisions. In fact, it leads away from community to a personal poverty that destroys.

This torn social fabric causes new generations to fall through the cracks. Poverty that leads to destruction is not the lack of personal wealth. That sort of lack can be answered in an instant. Poverty that leads to destruction is lack of vision or restraint. True poverty is flailing action that doesn't build on the future. It is the lack of self-control that calls the diabetic poor to just a few more calories. It is the lack of judgment that encourages one more theft instead of one more hour at work or study. Poverty that leads to destruction is rooted in the heart and soul. It is spurred on by whether a community cares or doesn't care. It is spurred on by whether the community plans or doesn't plan.

Poverty that leads to destruction is based in lack of being cared for or intentionally thought about. Fewer and fewer people watch out for the souls of individuals in their communities. Children who are brought up without grandparents, aunts, uncles, long-term friends of the family, or anyone who will take on these roles, are children robbed of social wealth. We have taken the blessing of family and given it to institutions. We have thrown away the humanity from a society that doesn't think that it has time to share. A society of individuals unconcerned with others produces the kind of destructive poverty that money alone will never fix. An institution might find a way to heal your body or educate you, but an institution can never build a soul.

Poverty's destructive elements must be again addressed through healthy relationships with people with

19

godly perspectives. Wherever poverty has destroyed, love has not done its job. The church has missed her opportunity to care for the desperate by not identifying with the desperate. Identifying with the poverty that calls people to care for others (sacrificially, even) can surely be endured just like braces in a child's mouth. Poverty that grows character and feeds the soul can actually heal. It is that pocket of poverty that calls the church to be rich in faith (James 2). It is poverty that teaches us to pray, allows us to forgive our neighbors, and ask that God's will be done on earth as it is in heaven. Through Christ's servitude He identified with the poor (Philippians 2). So can we. When we learn to care for the poor, to go beyond the topsoil and get to the roots, the sprouting roots that cause the hunger of the soul, we can once again become our brothers' keepers.

COMPETITIVE

You should know that despite being poor, we are competitive. And we're man and woman enough to admit it.

For years, the men in our extended families have said that Jim could play basketball if he cared. He never has and we don't think he ever will. Games, like basketball, are an opportunity to talk. These games, like most other activities, are an occasion to share stories, to build relationships.

It's not winning games that drive us to be competitive, but spiritual reward that fuels our competition. *Scripture* promises gold, silver, precious stones, crowns, the responsibility to reign over cities as Jesus reigns over all creation for those who care for others. Hearing the words "well done" will be worth the time, energy, sacrifice, and humility we spend in caring for others. Forceful men are taking the kingdom by force. We are those people. We have a goal and we play to win.

Jim's twin sister used to have a button that read "Presently Seeking A Country To Rule." Ours would read "Presently Working For The Privilege Of Ruling A City In The Future." It's not as catchy, but it gets the point across. We are unable to meet a stranger without wondering if he is the least of Jesus' brethren or if he might be an angel. In fact, we have met Michael the archangel once. He told us. Really! His shoe size is larger than Jim's and he lives just past the railroad tracks off Sherman. The least of these, angels unaware, strangers in the land, these people are our cup of tea. We are never happier than when we can get a group of strangers together and enjoy their company.

We know missionaries who seek God's glory and are motivated by the fear of God. We know friends who have a reciprocal love for Jesus. We know people who have been forgiven much and are joyfully obligated. We know people who are moved by their existential relationship with God. Our motivation is encompassed by all these things, yet we are more motivated by reward than the others. We are so thankful that the Lord has built us all in different ways.

We are awestruck by the glory of God, but our primary motivation is captivated in a verse about Jesus: "for the joy set before Him, He endured the cross, despising the shame." Just as in the present world, in the future those who are extreme personalities with extreme ways will have extreme impact and extreme reward. They also can be extremely irritating. We have met that sort ourselves. Our goal is to be extreme for the love of God, and in the way we love others.

God expects us to care for people. We know this from the New Testament as well as the Old. I Timothy tells us to be hospitable. Isaiah 58 tells us to care for the stranger in the land. Multiple passages tell us to care for those who are new to the area. We enjoy doing all of those. We even enjoy doing them in big ways.

We became friends with a young lady who had become the closest friend and confidant of a new refugee community. She was finishing her social work degree and entered an internship that cared for the new refugees coming into our city. They had been here a matter of months and she wanted them to experience a traditional Christian Thanksgiving. Our friend was having trouble organizing such a large group. We were able to make things easy and are so glad we did. We had forty Palestinians at Thanksgiving dinner that year. We shared a meal and fellowship with these new friends and others. That day we enjoyed fellowship with friends from ten different countries, if you count Mississippi. This year we had lots of people for Thanksgiving, almost seventy, and we'd be thrilled if there were more next year. Our competitive streak is showing again.

One of the present rewards of this drive to serve has been the many friendships we have experienced. But even greater has been the breadth of experiences our children have experienced. Our children rightly call us crazy, sometimes obsessive. Can you believe that? They laugh at the multiplicity of cultures we expect them to engage with as we pursue friendships. They have learned to weep with those who weep, but more often than not they have rejoiced with those who rejoice. Our children have found that it is easy to give thanks to God when surrounded by refugees who find themselves safe for the first time in their lives. It makes sense to them that their new country makes a point of giving thanks to God every November. Our children have seen the love of God expressed with food, caring and conversation translated so everyone can laugh. They are blessed in ways we wish everyone could be. By seeking to create a large circle of love that cares for the stranger, the refugee, the one new in this land, we and our children have had a glimpse of heaven where every tongue, tribe, and nation will be before the throne of God. Although the ultimate reward will be in heaven, by pursuing it now we experience a foretaste of that joy here on earth!

QUESTIONS FOR REFLECTION:

How has God already equipped you for ministry?
How could you adapt your ministry to those who are in need?
Is poverty earned or deserved?
What suffering is God calling you to?
How does God use suffering in the world?
How could we again be our brother's keeper?
In what ways did God build you to obey Him?

CHAPTER 2

FRIENDS AND NEIGHBORS

Six Charles at Church
Player
I Need an Exorcist
Elmer
Overcomers
Overheard

THE SIX CHARLES AT CHURCH

We often have shortage of many things at Neighborhood Fellowship, but we have never had a shortage of men named Charles.

Charles the Former Biker has been both the scariest man we have ever known and the source for eighteen years of some of our greatest stories. He trains his friends in the wisdom of the street and watches out for us the way a biker tempted to call up a troop of vigilantes might.

If we express that someone has wronged us, Charles is willing to provide whatever service might be required to make it right. One day, he showed us one of the tattoos on the inside of his mouth. He said that the "other one," the one that can be seen only when he pulls up his upper lip, "had to be earned."

These tattoos are all part of his past life, along with the tattoo of tear drops down his cheeks and the myriad of others over his body. We began our relationship with Charles when he worked as a painter on our house before our church began. We became friends when we buried his poodle after a short and eventful service. Charles grew ever dearer to us as his faith ignited and he literally caught fire on the way to his baptism, but that's another story. For Jim, Charles has been both a bodyguard and a teacher. And now a righteous man, Charles brings an interesting crowd to church and leads them in knowing the Lord. We have gone through more sadness with Charles than any other friend and we are comforted by the Scripture that says, "He who is forgiven much loves much."

Charles the Disabled Musician is a stately man with stories of leading bands and playing guitar throughout the Midwest and eastern Canada. His hands are arthritic. His speech has a slur to it, indicative of palsy, but he doesn't say what he suffers from. His stories are lucid and his smile lights the room. He walks a bit like Charlie Chaplin, stiff-legged with a rocking from side to side. He is usually looking for a cup of coffee, so we keep a pot on with him in mind. He greets us together, something Debbie appreciates. He is like a friend with a deep understanding of who we are as a couple, even though we have only known him a few years. We ask about his children; he tells us short stories about them or his music. When we talk, it is always about the beauty of things tangible. We are always happier when we have had a few minutes to talk with Charles. He is struggling with getting around more than before, but he is still gracious in his relationships. We pray for his health and look forward to seeing him regularly.

Charles the Emotional came to the clinic with his friend. They were both homeless in that absolute way. They behaved like buddies, like two old men having their free senior coffee at McDonald's. Both used to watch out for each other and continued to warn each other about the consequences of their drinking. Charles pledged to come to our drug and alcohol freedom meeting. He didn't make it. I reminded him and he told me that if someone would just pick him up, he would come. We tried that, too. Charles is now among the disappeared. He is gone and rumored dead. His buddy is confined to a nursing home.

Many days another Charles would greet us with the list of how many days he was in the county lockup. Charles was offended if we wouldn't get him food right away. He took correction well, but was struggling to implement the things he must do. He was sweet and traded on his winning sincerity by adding it to an endearing smile. When he was mostly sober, he would avoid becoming saccharine in his appreciation for help. But when he had a snootful, we just wanted to get away from him. Sadly, he doesn't visit us anymore. His death was a sad blow to us.

Charles the Early Bird comes to see what good things might be available to those who come to church.

Charles the Run Over and Yellow hasn't been to the church building this year. Charles was glad to see us when he came. We cared, but we were honest. Each time we saw him we told him that we were surprised he was still alive. He got skinnier and skinnier, looking more like Gollum from "Lord of the Rings." He was endearing because of his all but unintelligible speech. He pointed at his leg or his arm, showed us the new hospital tag and began telling us about being recently hit by a car, truck, or train. It was a charm all Charles' own. He spoke and less than a quarter of the words could be understood. Yet every inflection and every self-amusement was put into this speech. He pointed. He laughed. We hugged. He had things to say but no more the ability to say them. He called Jesus "JC" and continued to pour out thanksgiving and praise for the great "JC" who was with him. He gave testimony at church and praised God that he was still alive. At least that's what we think he said. It turns out that he has died as well.

PLAYER

We nickname people until we can get their names in our memories. Player was stylin' as they say around Tenth Street. He was too old to wear the tracksuit and Yankees ball cap. His body was emaciated and his skin withered. Some white hair was among those sprouting on his shaved head. Yet he was attempting the air of a young man with power. His hat sat sideways. Yes, he was a man of connection who just might be able to get you anything you wanted, anything.

Even though he was dressed as understated street power, he was in need. He smelled of yesterday's drinking binge and was hoping that the church could supply him with some groceries.

It isn't our habit to put people off, but Player was the exception that proves the rule. After the usual sermon that comes with food from the pantry, Jim was under the impression that Player was probably a Christian that the Lord was dealing with. We knew that people in his apartment building had just come for food. They would share with him and he wouldn't starve. Jim told him to come back the next day for church and then we would load him up. This was unusual. We have a meal on Sundays following the service and opening the food pantry would overwhelm everything we do in worship, teaching, and fellowship.

Sunday came and Player was in the service. He had left most of his street attitude at home. After the service and during the meal, he told one of the responsible older men that they were supposed to get him food. Knowing that this was not our Sunday plan, they immediately questioned the situation. Jim disengaged from what he was doing to help. When we gave Player the food, he was tearful and expressive in his thanks. He said that the preacher knew just what he needed to hear and that he would be back. He thanked everyone in earshot on his way out.

He has been back and we have gotten to know him over these last few years. He is going to church with his older sister in the neighborhood. He is now just another friend with a real name, one we need not mention.. We expect God's blessing on him as he seeks both God's kingdom and His righteousness. We saw him last month and he is doing much better. We are glad to see our friend in the neighborhood. We rejoice in the Lord and expect a bright future for anyone who will humble themselves to receive the Word of God, even an older player.

"I NEED AN EXORCIST"

It was one of those days that seemed to pile up on itself. We had to go two ways to get the same goal. Our foster-daughter had a visit and we had chairs coming to the church building at the same time. Jim had most of the children. They were not excited about the reason we were at the church building. We had organized our world the best we could to get the three hundred used chairs down to the basement stage. It was just our family and the elderly couple who do delivery for our inner-city church. The truth is that they are only elderly if you count age as their seventy plus years would suggest. They travel, continue to haul freight around the country, and on most occasions can outwork the fittest in our clan. So as we were waiting for the chairs to come, Jim was herding the kids, like a man does, or as one herds cats. When he turned around, he saw a young man dressed in a green army coat we had only met once or twice. This future friend saw that the church door was open so he came in at the most inopportune time. He found Jim correcting the kids.

"Can I talk to you privately?" were the first words out of this young man's mouth. Jim's head fell to his chest. These words are usually code for "I'm going to waste your time with some tragic story and then expect money, lots of money." Although this was not the right time as the chair-moving ministry was scheduled, Michael had actually come to the right place. So Jim shooed the children into another room and told him he only had a few minutes. This young man said, in soft tones, "I need an exorcist." By this time, the two were seated in the hallway and Jim asked, "How do you know?"

"They keep me up at night. They kick my bed! They turn the TV on in the middle of the night! They keep me up by saying that I'm lazy."

Jim asked how he knew that it was demons. Michael said that it was his first memory from childhood. He said that he wasn't afraid of them, but they were such an irritation. Sometimes they would come, sometimes they would go, but he knew that it was spirits that were shouting at him. He wanted relief!

Jim told him that he would be glad to pray and that all this activity seemed to be outside his body so it might just be the case of spiritual oppression. Michael said no, he had a demon in his stomach that talked to him. This demon was causing him so many problems that he had gone to the doctors who were looking for the stomach problem with some kind of a scan. He said, "They think I'm schizophrenic."

Jim replied that some people are schizophrenic and some are demon-possessed and some are both. Michael nodded. "Let's deal with the easier one first. If it's demons, they will respond to prayer and your desire to be free."

But before they prayed, Jim warned him of the passage in Luke 11. The man who sent his demonic spirit away, cleaning up his spiritual house, only to have that spirit return with seven more worse than the original. This young man said that he had never heard of that passage, so Jim explained that if he wanted extended deliverance that he needed to have Christ in that place and that he would be served well if he read Scripture and regularly gathered with the church. He agreed just as the chairs arrived. The kids and Debbie began to carry. Jim began to pray. With each set of three or five chairs we could hear Jim, louder and more confident.

"In Jesus' name," was the refrain. More chairs and more prayer, then the two of them, Jim and this young man, appeared from the hallway ready to work. No cry for money. No extended excuses why the exorcised man couldn't carry.

Both Jim and he carried down man-sized loads. He was so appreciative he carried more, and then he left. Jim told Michael that if the prayer was somehow inadequate that he should come back to church on Sunday where a group would pray and some would fast and together they would see what the Lord would do.

As for us, we saw a fearful man come into the building and a man who was not afraid to labor leave the building.

That might be enough evidence of deliverance for us. But he was just the first of six disturbed people we dealt with that day, two schizophrenics, one crack-addicted prostitute, one simple woman who can't count, and a visiting "eternal son of God" who is receiving revelation daily. Only a few wanted freedom.

HENRY

We regularly complain about the things not taught to us at Moody Bible Institute. We were taught wonderfully practical skills for ministry, how to lead worship, and how to put together Bible studies of all kinds. We were even taught to cross cultures and write down unrecorded languages. But there are a few holes in our education that would have been useful to fill in while we were young.

We never learned how to get a restraining order.

We are self-taught in the areas of locksmithing.

We don't remember hearing about being conflicted while doing the right thing. We expected doing the right thing would yield peace.

Our church doesn't have hours like most places. If someone is hungry then they probably didn't schedule that hunger for a particular day of the week or time. We believe that if someone is in need, that we should do our best to address the need in the moment. There can be extenuating circumstances, but for the most part we try to help.

This view of ministry is terribly inconvenient. However, it keeps us from saying to Jesus, or the least of His brothers, "Come back between the hours of ten and two, the second Tuesday of the month."

From time to time, because other groups do food pantry on a set schedule, we will have a run of people wanting food. People who are new to relationship with us will think that we are handing out free food and that they better hurry. The truth is, we are, but it's a lot more complicated than it sounds. Each person is immediately invited into a relationship with us, the church, and the Lord. Many receive help the first time, but shrink back from asking again.

We look at our food pantry like so many of our ministries. These kindnesses are a response to God's command to love our neighbor as ourselves. When we are hungry, we are hungry in the moment. It is also a platform to talk to those in need about their greatest need, a relationship with a loving God. We do our best to explain the love of God and the responsibility Christians have to obey the Lord and seek His kingdom first. It is this conversation that most give assent to, and then don't want to have again. Those who don't want the religious part often don't come back for food from the church.

After just such a run on our food pantry, a man we'll call Elmer was number eleven in line one afternoon. Jim gave him "the spiel" as he calls it. Just as Jim had told the previous ten, we were glad to help but we were more concerned about souls than bellies and at some point in the future we would press them regarding their intention concerning the Lord.

Most received this revelation with some entertainment. It is funny how honest poverty culture can be. Henry, though, had been around multiple times. Repeatedly he had asked for groceries, come to the clinic, and had a hot cup of coffee and a sandwich there. But he wouldn't darken the doorway of one of our church services. Jim pressed him as to why he wouldn't join us at church. He asked, "How many times do I have to get saved?"

That was something we hadn't heard before! Why did he ask that? Jim pressed him in regard to growing in Christ. Jim went through the passages that tell us to grow in our relationship to the Lord and His church. Henry seemed amazed that there was more than "getting saved." He asked if the service had children in it. Jim was chagrined at this prejudice against children. It seemed so incongruent with poverty culture and most people's joy at seeing children in church. "Of course we have children! They are our future. Why do you ask?"

Henry said "I'm on a list."

We are watchful and have tried to help men like this before. We are conflicted as we consider Elmer's need for spiritual growth, and the children's need for protection. In our experience, these men who have made it on a sexual predators list are predators who will not be satisfied with anything less than opportunity for evil. The Scripture tells us that it would be better to have a millstone hung around our necks and cast into the sea than to offend one of these little ones. We take our care for our children very seriously. So we have a plan for those on "a list." The men of the church have a special class for such offenders. They are invited to a local fast-food restaurant where we study the Scripture. We can be the church without ever putting a child at risk. Henry wasn't interested in that.

OVERCOMERS

One of our friends named Doug, a wild man if you have ever known one, was at his church in Sheridan, Indiana, when Jim was speaking one Sunday morning several years ago. Jim sought out Doug and said, "When are you going to start that Overcomers meeting downtown?"

Neighborhood Fellowship has needed a drug and alcohol recovery group for years, but most of our leaders have been called to ministry by God in our youth. We were not the crowd to look someone in the eye and know whether they are lying about their addictions. Doug has experienced a lot of the hardness of addiction and he had the experience to set another right. But Doug had lots of excuses, including the distance of a 40-minute drive. He was already caring for another group in his own county. He had plenty to do between his two jobs, family, and church. He didn't want to start the next Overcomers class when someone else should do it. There was no way that Doug should be the person who should start the class.

Most of a year went by when Doug and a companion named Brady came to our elders and said they would like to start a class. They had been to the jails in their county and most of the people locked up there are from our county. Many inmates would say to Doug, "Where is the meeting I can go to when I get out?"

Doug was ashamed to say there was no such meeting. So, under conviction, Doug and Brady began their class. Paul, a disabled veteran who is part of Neighborhood Fellowship, began attending. He was the only one who began attending. But the three of them were faithful, week after week after week. It seemed like no one else was going to join, but it was clear that there was a great need on our street. From time to time, the elders would joke with the tiny class that they had cured the problem of addiction on Tenth Street. Yet, Tenth Street is full of trouble, drug dealing, prostitution, all sorts of corruption. If there was ever a place that an Overcomers meeting should be well attended, Tenth Street was the place, but week after week it was just the three of them.

Judy had been coming to Neighborhood Fellowship for five years or more. She was simple. Her drinking was out of control. She was a tiny lady in her 50s who needed direction, help, and encouragement. One July, Judy decided to give up drinking. We immediately encouraged her to join Overcomers for support. She didn't think she needed them, but after three or four weeks of sobriety she began to go to the meetings. She grew ever more faithful to church and the class.

While at Overcomers, she heard the Word of God as it related to her drinking. She heard about sobriety from people who had experienced the same addiction she had been involved with. Judy felt at home, but we had no sense of what God was doing. God had given Judy a heart for evangelism. She was compassionate and began to call in all her friends. After a few weeks of Judy being at the Overcomers meeting, we looked in and saw that there were about 20 people in the meeting, all of Judy's friends. Although they have gone through some lean times, these four and others are faithful and growing.

Judy wasn't able to express all that she had found in Overcomers, but the people that she had shown compassion with over the years knew that Judy only wanted their good, so they came to the meeting.

We rejoiced to see the work of God. We rejoiced to see His gifting. We rejoiced to know that the Lord uses the simple things of this world to confound the wise. Judy's ministry continues. Somehow, whether by the direct work of the Holy Spirit or the encouragement of her leaders, she decided that she would no longer be a taker. Judy decided that she would be a giver. She just wanted to know when the children at school needed their lunch. Since that time she has continued serving. It doesn't matter what is needed. She's just glad to do something, even if it is making the coffee, or some of the cleaning..

Doug, Brady, Paul, and Judy have taken the thing that at one time they were most ashamed of and turned it into a platform for the Gospel and good works. They saw there was no one else to do the work so they stepped up. In doing so they have communicated once again that we "can do all things through Christ who strengthens me."

"God can use all things for good for those who love Him and are called according to His purpose." These friends used their skills, experiences and concern for others to the level that every Christian should consider.

THINGS OVERHEARD FROM FRIENDS AND NEIGHBORS

"That's the last time I let a convicted murderer move in with me."
A young man in our community surprised that his roommate had anger control issues.

"You have a real child problem around here."
A suburban friend glancing over the number of children in our service.

"Money is not for food."
A woman very accustomed to receiving government assistance.

"Yeah, I'm an addict and a thief. But I'm still a good dad."
A friend describing his parenting after being confronted about his addictions.

"It's just like camping."
A schizophrenic friend describing his life in homelessness.

"If you're not worried about your soul, we're not worried about your belly."

Jim's stance on giving food to those who continually avoid church.

"Beggars can't be choosers."
Things said when the quality of stuff given is low.

"We were the good bad guys."
A friend's explanations of the biker life.

"They left half a perfectly good bucket of lard in the alley. Can you believe that? So I took it home."
Another schizophrenic friend after a great find.

"And then my guts fell out! They just fell out! I thought I was going to die!"
Friend's explanation of the enormous scar on his stomach.

"He was on fire when he came to the door. We put him out and we still have a spot in the yard."
What it is like living across the street from a schizophrenic friend.

"I preferred the tube top wedding."
Debbie after Jim performed a wedding where the couple had tattooed on their rings.

"They'll never take me alive! Let's lock ourselves in here."
Addicted friend said this as Jim was in his house and six police cars pulled up to the door.

"Mary, why are you growing pot on your front porch?"
Neighbor asking Jim's mother about the plant on the front porch that she had nursed to health.

"She's the preacher's ol' lady."

Neighbor describing who Debbie was.

"They should just hose down the prostitutes over there."
A realtor suggesting how Tenth Street might deal with its prostitution issue.

"I have my name tattooed on my chest, so in case I get my head blowed off they won't have to wake my mother at three in the morning."
A friend who was explaining the large tattoo on his chest.

"This just isn't convenient for our people."
An explanation why one of the largest churches in Indianapolis would no longer be helping.

"Paint is not a toy."
An explanation to any group that does physical work in the building.

"Go home and get your father's socks."
A clinic doctor's instruction to one of our children.

"Which would you rather have—a three-year-old building or a three-hundred-year-old building?"
The question posed to the Neighborhood Fellowship elders when our building was at risk.

"Weed, W-E-E-D, I know what that is. It's what momma smokes!"
Third-grader at NF confronted with a new spelling word.

"I'm going to shoot that gangsta."
A testimony given during the church praise service.

"I'm hanging on. You do the same"
Words of encouragement between two depressed people at a worship service.

"Oh yeah, I've got your name tattooed on my butt."
An explanation of how one of our more colorful friends wins a bet with his "your name" tattoo.

"What is the opposite of monogamy?"
An explanation of how one of our neighbors built community with his friends.

"Expended and Suspelled"
The common condition of students who are no longer welcome in the public schools.

"Doin' life by installments"
A lifetime criminal's description of the repeat offender's career path.

"There are those you pick up last and drop off first, no matter what."
Advice from a church bus driver for handling some kids.

"I praise God that He saved this no-good, rotten sinner"
The regular testimony of the same church bus driver about himself.

QUESTIONS FOR REFLECTION:
How can people in need be generous?
How do you know what God wants you to do in a difficult moment?

What things that you are ashamed of could God use to help others?

What does deliverance look like in your ministry?

How do you protect children and still minister?

Are you too busy to hear God?

Can you find humor in ministry?

CHAPTER 3

GIVING AND RECEIVING

Stuff is only the Beginning
The Lone-Ranger Giver
We Got a House?!
Wheeling and Dealing God's Way

STUFF IS ONLY THE BEGINNING

In our ministry we deal with stuff. Stuff can be useful. In fact, hand-me-downs are the things that friendly families and caring neighbors are known for. These things that survived their first use, stretch the second users' budgets, and can even become precious because of their association with the giver.

Old stuff is often useful. It fits with the kind of brotherly love that we often hear older generations speak of, when they praise a time or town where neighbors were concerned about the welfare of others.

Odd new stuff can be passed about. These generosities are brotherly kindnesses that are the beginning of love. Just as love pledged at the altar with "I do" is just the beginning, a beginning that should be talked about and celebrated, so giving should have a beginning that grows into an ever-strengthening commitment.

Yes, brotherly love that shares its extras should always abound. It should be recognized as the beginning of love. This should be the common place love that pervades our homes and churches and is restored in the American culture. It should also be seen as the beginning of our love for others that grows with maturity into a passion that demands that we lay down what we have, as well as our very lives, for others and for our God. This maturity is the place where loving our neighbor as ourselves is achieved.

In the Old Testament, gleaning, where food was left to be harvested by hardworking poor folk (Leviticus 23), was the very same food that was harvested for the more affluent. There was no difference in quality between food for the affluent and food for the poor.

Giving a cup of cold water to a disciple (Matthew 10:42), giving the widow's mite (Luke 21:2) when it is all you have, comes with great reward. Giving stuff can be the work of God (Exodus 25:1-7).

We've had a wide assortment of experiences in our ministry with the poor when it comes to the things people give. One time, 240 pounds of Fruit Loops came to our church. It was in one box and we couldn't get it the front door. We gave Fruit Loops to every possible neighbor. We were Fruit Loop evangelists. We filled trash bags with these sweet circles and we gave. This effort to organize the church to distribute what people liked was less difficult than the organization necessary for other things—clothes, furniture, vegetables, medical supplies, office supplies, building materials.

Everything imaginable has come our way for distribution. Some things have been what our poor neighborhood could use at just the right time. Sometimes old stuff has been desirable for its style. Sometimes it has filled in where there was lack. We have seen older medical equipment shipped to poorer areas that benefited from the upgrade.

While we are appreciative of the generosity of others, some of the gifts haven't always been, well, useful. At times, they can even appear to be someone else's unwanted leftovers.

Sometimes the flood of unwanted leftovers, or even wanted ones, is of such a magnitude that they require considerable administrative abilities, which are a luxury ministries to the poor often do not have. When stuff is given without the framework of a relationship that understands the people and the people's needs, then the stuff becomes a mound of assorted goods that demands hands to sort, organize and deliver. The ministry infrastructure can't handle the load of stuff or find a place for the particular item. The product expires, molds, or can't be used without great expense, and soon it is in the dumpster.

Sometimes the giving is of such a nature that people on the receiving end will spend a lot of time on stuff, and chances are that time should have been spent on something else.

The emphasis in giving must be on the people involved. Christ is present in both givers and receivers. God makes His presence known as we give to the needs of others. He is honored when we have the right attitude about giving. It is also a joy to give. "It is more blessed to give than receive" (Acts 20:35). And God is also at work through those on the receiving end. He is actively exalting the humble and answering the prayer of the needy.

Old stuff can be useful to people who have little, but giving unwanted leftovers that should probably have been given to the scrap pile, is not the same as giving an offering to the Lord. Throughout the Scripture, God demanded the best and the first (Malachi 1:6-9). It is only when we give the best we have that the Lord receives our gifts as giving to Him. Many donate the things that they are done with—things that are subpar, have missing pieces or no longer function well.

May we gently point out that the flood of gifts to the needy do not include a glut of new leather couches or 80-inch plasma TVs. It might just be possible that giving things that are "good enough" in brotherly love must eventually grow to giving the very things we ourselves want.

Giving money isn't always the answer either. Solomon says with tongue in cheek that money is the answer to all things (Ecclesiastes 10:19). But it is only the answer if it is used for the purposes given.

All of us have given money. And those of us who have given money for the care of the poor know that there are issues as to administrative costs. The gift of cash might make it into the hands of the poor we hoped would be helped, but is more likely paying a middleman to attempt to care for the poor. Scripture teaches us that money is just a tool. Judas was rebuked for his view of money while the unscrupulous steward was praised for his ability to use money to gain relationships (Luke 16:1-9).

We must be wise when it comes to our giving and ask Biblical questions. Does our giving honor God? Does our giving fit Biblical patterns? Does our giving look like God's generosity? Is our giving maturing and becoming a reflection of loving our neighbor as ourselves?

When we give, we should make it personal and take the time to find just the right receiver. When we give things, we must consider the additional cost that comes with finding just the right home. Whatever we do, we must mature our giving to the level that our gifts are both an honor to God and a real help to the receiver.

THE LONE-RANGER GIVER

The Apostle Paul instructs his disciple Timothy to tell those who are rich in this world's goods to be generous and share. We have seen that sharing. Over the years we have experienced the loving arms of the larger Indianapolis church expressing a godly generosity as well as a humble dignity. Individuals, families, and occasionally organized church groups have stepped up to that purpose. We are blessed to see Christ in the giving and receiving of material goods. When individual generosity is hand-in-hand with the other commands of God, things are made more beautiful. The wonder of "on earth as it is in Heaven" is fulfilled.

May God bless the church leaders and Sunday School teachers who have taught those who have to give. May God bless the giver as well. We have seen individuals act like Christ. We have seen individuals give to institutions. We are well acquainted with men of means and social position who step forward for the good of many. These modern philanthropists are the very people who have influenced our culture to greatness.

And yet, we have also experienced giving of a different sort. It is a form of giving that comes from individuals who claim to represent "the church" but have no real sense of belonging, little affinity, and even less respect for their church and the leadership of their church. These individuals claim connection to a particular congregation—until their congregation somehow disappoints them. And then they claim connection to another congregation. Until that congregation disappoints them.

The one who insists on always giving and acting independently of the protection and accountability of a church sometimes casts ill effects. Our ministry has often found itself counting on the word of some generous giver who somehow forgot to follow through. These givers get excited in the moment and make a rash pledge. Disappointment is added to the grinding circumstances of the poor. Resentment is not far behind. And a root of bitterness may then spoil the faith of those chosen to be rich in faith. We have waited for years on some individual donors' pledges that have yet to materialize.

Autonomous giving, money and gifts given independently of a larger church body, are terrific in an emergency type situation. Such giving funds groups, which care for the needy in times of natural disaster. There is no time for a committee to form when a tsunami has struck. It is part of one's Christian duty to give in such circumstances. If an individual is unable to operate in the moment with God's compassion, then the love of God does not dwell in him.

One might think that we, of all people, would be thankful for the opportunity to point out our newest emergency and have compassionate people dig into their pockets. We are surrounded daily by the emergencies that poverty, violence, illness, and societal brokenness bring. We have benefited directly from spur-of-the moment, autonomous giving.

Yes, giving in an emergency meets an emergency need, but thoughtful, planned, organized giving should be the prevailing plan of God's people. We believe organized giving is better handled with the advice of godly leaders who will not only one day give an account to God, but will see to the follow-through of pledges and promises.

Autonomous giving fosters an independence that fosters isolationism. The church is meant to function as a body, every member helping and working with the other members.

Autonomous giving can also awaken the darker side of ministries. It invites ministries to sell themselves, to compete for attention, to compete for sympathy, to compete for funds. We are good storytellers and could compete well in this arena, yet we refuse the thought of competition for funds in God's work. We see organizations that fundraise in this manner. We even see churches that have a "to the victor goes the spoils!" attitude. This attitude perpetuates a kind of fundraising that not only demeans the ministry, but defrauds the giver. The giver is no longer a friend who needs to be cared for like a friend. Neither is he a friend who happens to have resource. The giver becomes a resource that ministries compete for. The giver becomes a commodity. He is considered property of the receiver or his organization. The giver is won. He is not called by God or directed by the godly. He is wooed by man. And often exploited. The giver is talked about and praised. He often finds his name on a list or a building and is limited to the earthly reward an organization can give. This giver is robbed of his eternal reward and allows others to be taught to do the same. And if he has some view that his gifts have bought him access or influence, he can easily be angered when access or influence is not forthcoming.

There is great safety in giving in conjunction with the wisdom and guidance of a local church. Getting counsel from church leadership concerning giving is not blowing trumpets before you give your gift, nor does it mean you lose your reward in heaven. Getting informed and wise counsel concerning giving helps God's church stay on track, supports ministries that should be supported, and keeps the giver humble.

Practicing occasional lone-ranger giving when the need is pressing and the spirit compels is a sign of maturity, but consistent and planned giving under the guidance of the local church is maturity as well.

WE GOT A HOUSE?!

We are given many things besides clothing and food. Recently, we were given another house. A house! Another house! Is it a blessing? We don't know yet.

From time to time we are offered property. Sometimes it is offered to us as a family and sometimes to our church. This one is in the neighborhood, just a few blocks away from our house. It's been offered to us directly and since selling property is how we planned to subsidize our kids' college expenses, it has our attention. We have some rehab skills and have done such things before. We have transformed a four thousand dollar house into a twenty-five thousand dollar house with the help of what seemed to be a lot of money and unbelievable number of man hours. So maybe we should stick to our day jobs.

But the question regarding this present opportunity is, do we keep it? Do we share it? Or do we run away with all our strength? It's a really big job and there is no market right now for houses. The bleak reality is that our city has made it to number two on the empty/abandoned properties list. We are appalled at this societal problem and it again has become personal. It looks like this house will be a lot of work and no financial gain.

Some of our family members are selling houses. Maybe we could help the extended family. But not too long ago one of those family members was living in one of the houses we were unable to sell. The market has been such a wreck that this house won't be a blessing to anyone who doesn't have some time to wait. "What about a rental?" friends ask. But most of our church community has sworn off rentals. Who can throw families out on the street? So maybe we could give it to a young couple.

It is trashed. It needs a new roof, new windows, new siding and that is just what we can see from the outside.

We looked in the windows and it is fifty percent gutted. New plumbing and electrical are needed for sure. And who wants to live on a major thoroughfare? No one would pick this location unless it were cheap, or unless there were extenuating circumstances.

One friend asks if it comes with roaches? We can handle that. Lead paint and the desperate men who walk by seem to be the more permanent issue. We want to change the neighborhood for good, but the cost of time and money is pretty substantial. We don't have the money but that has always been the least of the problems. We have strong backs and willing hearts.

As we are considering the church community right now, we wonder if we all have the strength of relationship to make this an opportunity and not a disaster? Is this house a blessing or a curse? For some, "free" would answer that question. But we have had "free" so often that we can stand back and ask. Jesus' words are true, "It is better to give than receive." We will receive if this is a useful gift, not just a distraction.

Our family is not bad at fixing houses. Sometimes we even dial it up to eighty percent. We are eighty percent people when it comes to getting houses fixed. We have a long-term view about these dilapidated structures. We are just passing through these lands until the Lord returns and if you lower your standards, for now, you can be happier. We should improve whatever we touch but recognize that the buildings and lands are not truly permanent. Our house is a platform for ministry. Yes, some of "home" is lived out in our house but home is wherever the two of us get a chance to sit down and talk. So we may not give the usual advice when it comes to home ownership. We could easily entrap a young family with a long life of work.

A free house! Built by the community. If we are the urban Amish, which from time to time we claim, shouldn't we consider a barn raising/rehab for all the young families? Many have come to help with all their idealism. Could a house be their reward? Or should the reward be for those who have lived through trouble first? All these questions and little resource.

We will talk to the leaders of the church. We will see if we are the Amish. We will all have to see if we can put our hand to the work. We'll see, and hopefully not get tired. This will play out as God gives wisdom. Time will tell.

WHEELING AND DEALING GOD'S WAY

It may seem like we are overly concerned about the manner in which giving is done. We *are* concerned. Our concern is that when giving is practiced outside the boundaries of Scripture —giving freely, giving cheerfully, giving of your best, giving thoughtfully, giving under the umbrella of, and in conjunction with, local church leadership—we miss out on the blessings God intended.

We hold ourselves to the same standard of doing things God's way. One of our most memorable opportunities to practice God's plan for giving, receiving and conducting business transactions was years ago when we were first starting ministry.

We had just gotten back from working as missionaries in South Africa. Our child, a precious little girl, was about to experience her first winter in Indiana. How were we going to care for this little one? Our car, an ancient Fiat, was about fifteen years beyond cute and twenty-five years beyond new. It suited us as a get-around car but it barely had a back seat and it didn't have a heater. When Abigail was born we installed rear seat belts but had to put the roof down just to get her infant car seat in or out of the back. In short we owned a tiny hooptie that was guaranteed to freeze our newborn.

Jim worked at a service station at the time. It was less than a mile from home. There were people who loved cars around the station. They commented on our Fiat Spider. It wasn't long before everyone knew we were looking to trade for a car with a heater. After lots of talk one younger man said he always wanted an Italian convertible and would like to trade his Grand Am with a posi-tract rear end for our car. We were only concerned about having heat.

An old car has lots of problems. Jim wrote out three legal pad pages of the problems he knew the Fiat had. This young man wanted this little sports car so bad he could taste it. We wanted a heater. What a funny world. We exchanged titles and began driving. We were happy the young man was happy. All was well for four days. On the fourth day the new Fiat driver fell out of love and asked if we could trade back. He had driven the car hard and popped some tires. He didn't like it that the stick shift would sometimes come right out of the floor. He had changed his mind. We responded kindly but gave him little hope that we were interested in the new deal. We told him that we had been clear about the condition of the car and that we were satisfied with what we had gotten in the deal. We said that we would think about it and give him an answer in the next two days. The very next day we received a phone call from the young man's lawyer stating that we had misrepresented the 1976 Fiat 124 Spider. We asked if his client had shown him the three pages. The lawyer said that he had seen the list of problems with the car and suggested that we had still misrepresented the car. We were sad and angry but had one question for the lawyer. Was it his client's intention to sue us if we didn't trade back? His answer was yes! That took the decision from what we thought was right to what the Scripture says.

In the Sermon on the Mount, Jesus tells those who are on their way to court to make a deal along the way because they don't know what the judge will do. Jesus also says in that same passage that if someone demands your coat that you should give them your tunic (outer garment) as well. That young man ended up with both cars and both titles and we were now walking. This was not the plan for success that we had, but we didn't know how to reconcile God's commands and our lives any other way. The young man was not a Christian and could not conceive of any reason we would do this. We tried to explain and all he could do was to say "cool" and enjoy both cars. We did not enjoy our walks in the snow. We felt foolish for our part in the original trade. All we could do is bear the consequence and cry out to God, whose commands were making us more than a little frustrated.

Soon people in our church heard about our situation. Most responded with approval that we had followed our understanding of the passages. After a few weeks, one responded by giving us a car. We were blessed. It had a heater. Soon others offered us their spare cars saying they wanted to find a needy family to give them to and they were wondering if we could pass them along.

More than twenty years later we have been given over eighty sets of keys to as many cars. Jesus also says in Mark 10:30 that if we give up anything for the kingdom of heaven we will receive one hundred times as much and eternal life to come. And we no longer wonder what the Lord is doing when He asks us for obedience or a moment of suffering. By the way, through a strange set of circumstances we now have a 1971 Fiat Spider that needs a heater.

QUESTIONS FOR REFLECTION:
Does your giving fit Biblical patterns?
How can giving ever hurt the ones you are giving to?
Who helps you decide where you are going to give?
Are you glad to give in an emergency?
How do you measure giving, dollars, time, skill?
If a ministry is missing administration, should you give it anything?
Do God's commandments trump everything else? Can you give examples in your life?

CHAPTER 4

FOOD IS LOVE

The Food Pantry
Sunday Meal
Footnotes on Food

THE FOOD PANTRY

Anyone in a ministry that starts a house church or an outreach in an impoverished area knows, "Food is love." People are often in need and they recognize that they can get food at many ministries. The problem with that is there is a culture of dependency that has been brought on as families collapse, government provides more and more assistance, and ministries give without a call to responsibility.

We have had friends in our community who have said, "Money ain't for food." We are chagrined at that destructive thought pattern. But truly, there are people that are hungry, and their children can bear no personal responsibility. When Neighborhood Fellowship started, we hung a sign on our house telling the hours of worship; people saw the sign as evidence that they could get help from the people inside. All hours of the day and night, people would knock on our door. Some would need to go to the hospital. Some needed help sorting out marital problems. Some wanted to talk. Some wanted prayer. Many wanted food.

One day a friend from Zionsville Fellowship came by our house when people were knocking on the door and asking for food. He had come to find a way to support our inner-city church plant. He showed up to help and see. And help and see he did.

When he saw that they were needing food, he said "You're giving away your food?"

We said, "What would you do?"

We were doing what we believed anyone in our circumstances would do. We saw hungry folk as neighbors and we looked around for the potatoes or bread or whatever extras we had. We brought the food to the door, prayed for whoever was there and then sent them on their way.

Our friend Mark and his family came from a more organized world than we do. He said, "Why don't I make a few phone calls and see if we can get a food pantry going?"

That food pantry has been going eighteen 18 years. Friends from Zionsville Fellowship and other churches have brought food all these years. It has been their hope that we would distribute it with some thoughtfulness, care, love and prayer.

We were glad to do this ministry, although we have always thought that those who aren't close enough to the needy to distribute food themselves are missing some of the greatest blessings that exist in the church. After twenty years, for the most part it is the same people distributing the food as it was in the first days. We wish more people could experience the blessing of ministering to the hungry personally. We don't want to be the "feeding specialists" or the professionals when it comes to feeding the poor. Giving food or money to Neighborhood Fellowship is certainly a first step to those who don't know how to start, but we hope it would be a first step followed by second and third steps.

We have always had a particular view on how giving food to the needy should play out. This particular view comes with the thought that if you love your neighbor as yourself, then you recognize that when you're in need, you didn't plan it. Hunger doesn't show up only on Tuesdays between ten and two and on Fridays from three to seven. We didn't want regimented hours for our food pantry where people would plan on "shopping" and Neighborhood Fellowship would be just another stop along their grocery gathering day.

We wanted our church community to be people of help and healing. Our church building, where we keep the donated food, needs to be a place where we can facilitate that goal. We call Neighborhood Fellowship's food pantry an emergency food pantry. It must be an emergency, if someone is willing to endure the short but pointed sermon that Jim gives before he gives out food. After giving food to our neighbors, we remind them that if they are not worried about their souls, then soon we would not be worried about their bellies. Most of the time, people giggle at hearing this, then they agree. After a second or third time, most people have appreciated being called to account. Before long, people feel like we might really love them. We invite them to church, where they know they should be anyway. And then we look at the Gospel of John, chapter fifteen, verse seven where the Lord says, "If you abide in me, and my word abides in you, ask whatever you will, and that will be done." When we remind people of these verses, we tell them they need to be in church, and they need to be reading God's Bible. For the most part, we get a good response, and more and more people fill the church building.

We don't think that we are developing what was called, two generations ago, "rice Christians," because although when they come to the church in need we try to meet the needs, there isn't more access to food just because they come to us. There is a call to responsibility; we question why people can't find work, we question what they're doing with their disability check, and soon we see those who had previously only been takers become givers.

If it were not for our friend Mark's kindness, we would probably still be giving out the groceries from our cabinets. That wouldn't be wrong, but more people have joined in, and we've been able to help more people. More have been helped nutritionally, as well as spiritually, than we ever could have helped as an individual family or even as a group of families.

We are so thankful for those who, once or twice a month, gather together food from Mark's church. Our friends Vince and Kent have taken on the regular responsibility. Now, individuals as well as institutions have added to the food bank. We are thankful for the widow who brings food to church. We are thankful for the 80-year-old truck driver and his wife who often carry the food to our building. We are thankful to our friends who organize the money to buy the food. Many have been found faithful.

Every individual Christian is commanded to love his neighbor as himself. Every church has the responsibility to distribute what the saints have to those who are in need. We're thankful to have this ministry, though we never consider the emergency food pantry the point of what we do. It is available when we have food. It is available when people can find us. It is often inconvenient to stop what we are doing to meet a need, but it is important.

However important it is, though, it cannot become our primary goal of ministry. It is a secondary work that points to the good news of relationship with Christ. Over the years, the food pantry has been helped and added to by engaging with other organizations, by the concerns of many individuals, and by people who were willing to give money. The food pantry is one of our favorite ways to invite people to church. It is an entry point to relationship. We see people treated as friends and neighbors. We have no hours, but relational people know how to find out who is giving help and when they can find it. Whoever comes to NF hears God's promise: "Seek first the kingdom of God and all these things shall be added to you."

SUNDAY MEAL

Our church has had a meal as part of all our Sunday services since the day we started to worship together. It is usually a simple meal but sometimes it is spiced with special celebrations for birthdays or holidays or times of plenty. It is a family meal that is rarely burdensome. We rejoice to spend a little more time together. We often say that it is easier getting to know one another over dinner than watching the back of each other's heads during a sermon. Our meal time is the beating heart of community building for the church.

The Sunday meal is also an opportunity for us to bring newcomers in and a time that shepherds can check on the congregations. If someone outside our community hears about Neighborhood Fellowship, that we have a 3:00 PM worship service with a meal, they often, even usually, ask if they could somehow help with the meal. These questions are a sign of Christian life but not necessarily a sign of Christian maturity. Many of those who want to help the poor are disadvantaged if they don't already live among people in need. Many don't live among the poor. In fact, the American dream includes trying *not to* and so God's command, that the rich in this world's goods must be generous and share and not neglect good works, is made inconvenient. It can involve traveling to other parts of a city or having to meet new people. Why do all that when sharing can be as easy as writing a check? It is often a kindness to send money to those who have little. But giving money does not finish anyone's responsibility unless good works go along with some of that money. Good works are not limited to helping those who are poor, but it is plain that God intends that His people care for those who have need, or are somehow oppressed, or at risk of being oppressed. God's lists of people who must be cared for are found in Isaiah 58, Matthew 25, and James 1.

Our church has been able to build a platform for those who live elsewhere to help at church gatherings. It is a mixed bag; some outsiders can do more harm than good with their attempts at doing good. I Corinthians 11 tells us that selfishness can ruin any meeting. For the most part, our plan has been a good beginning. These new helpers hear the word meal, and they usually think soup kitchen. It is inevitable that people imagine what they have seen in the media. It would better if people got their wisdom from the Scriptures, or serving with their own church. And for this reason the meal is guarded. It wasn't always guarded, but we have learned our lessons. We had to allow some relationships to go, though they got tired of us before we had to fire them. Now, we stop any volunteer, who is not already in relationship, and begin to explain our expected process. We say this is how to develop a relationship with the church. By the way, relationship is our goal. We explain carefully and deliberately:

"First come worship with us. Join with us in the singing and the teaching. Then you will understand a lot more about who we are. You will say "oh!" when you see the mix of people. When some of us come to church meetings, we look like suburban folk. Others are physically or mentally impaired, or might just look that way. (Our family has been mistaken as homeless on occasion.) Others are distressed. Some are unaccompanied children. We are an odd mix in a traditional church building. We are multi-racial, multi-ethnic, multi-lingual, multi-generational, multi-economic, and with different degrees of ability. We are a family. When you get through that part of your "oh" realization, then we invite you to eat with us. Many people cannot get through this hurdle. Preconceptions may make you feel as though you are taking food from hungry people. You are not! We have plenty. Some perceive our kitchen to be unsanitary. It is not! We have a health department approved kitchen and it gets better each year. Until you can eat with us, and fellowship around our beat-up tables, you can never see this time for what it is. It is a family gathering! We are all there for fellowship. Our meal is an extension of our worship. If you have gotten through those two hoops, then you can help serve or bring a meal. By the time you have identified with us through the sharing of food, you are ready to help serve dinner."

Some who want to help still hide behind the stainless steel tables. Others can't leave the kitchen. But most who come in order to serve find time to sit down and talk to the people they came to serve. Some who come to serve understand that in the giving and receiving, in the cooking and the serving, that they are giving to God. Others realize that we could have done this ourselves but they become thankful that we would share this opportunity. Those who understand are often the ones who bring something that they would serve their own families. Others see this gathering as the snapshot of what heaven will be like, with its great banquet. Some have added their good works to what they have given in money. Everyone who comes is seen by our Lord as trying to do good and taking the risks that are worthy of children of God. We hope you will, too.

FOOTNOTES ON FOOD

A SAUERKRAUT JUICE LAMENT

We went to one of the larger food banks that are open to smaller food pantry ministries. When we returned, other people at church who help give the food to the needy inspected the haul. They were not impressed. Jim said, "I didn't take any of the sauerkraut juice. Its existence is evidence that there are some salesmen who could sell ice to Eskimos." There were surprising deficiencies with this opportunity to do good. Ten percent of the food was out of date. That wouldn't have been difficult to sort through but the fact that the dated goods were jars of baby food added insult to injury. Out they went. Some of the other items could be useful, but a number of them leaned toward the bizarre. Should hungry stomachs complain? Maybe not, but maybe givers should be thoughtful. The children at church have figured out that we get the products that didn't have a chance at selling. This is a kind of brotherly sharing that doesn't meet the standard of loving our neighbor as ourselves. Inferno-flavored chips are the delicacy of the corner quickie food mart and Chai-flavored hot cereal wouldn't even sell well at the organic food market. These foods are not fare for an empty stomach that desires some comfort. We stopped going to the food bank.

LOVING YOUR NEIGHBOR AS YOURSELF

One of the churches that wanted to help us with our food pantry asked what people in the city needed. We answered protein. Starch floods the city. Mac and cheese, Top Ramen noodles, and bread are distributed by the case, but protein is expensive. Rare as hens' teeth. Canned meat, peanut butter, rice and beans, and soups are the places to start for those who are desperate. There is one particular church that has gone above and beyond. They buy their food at the same full-service grocery we shop at. They deliver the food to our building and, when they have time, they fill the food pantry themselves. They don't blow a trumpet to announce their good work. They helped first by listening, secondly by making things as easy on us as they could. Almost like clockwork, as the pantry grows empty, this generous church gives us good things we are proud to give to the hungry. These are friends who truly love their neighbors as themselves.

IT'S NOT EASY BEING ORANGE

Over the years our family has seen that food is love to the poor. It is true. Homeless, desperate folk, refugees, strangers, people passing through, children, old friends, all experience food offered in friendship as love. We love hospitality. We love giving and receiving. We love a crust of bread and a cup of coffee. Almost any time is time for a little snack, a cup of coffee or a cold glass of water and a conversation. We love people and people feel loved when there is food. We are hardly uppity when it comes to food either. We have dined on the simple cuisine of all parts of the world. We are humble in our resources and common in our upbringing. We have dined on raccoon, tripe, chicken feet, souse, and have eaten greens on three continents. We have made meals from rice and sugar as well as bits of potato. We know simple foods and like them. We also know fine desserts with calories enough to sustain a village. We love butter sauces and can name cheeses from fifty regions of Europe. We are well acquainted with food. Food is an emotional experience. And we praise God for its place in church life, family, and friendship.

That said, Jim struggles with his weight. He decided once that he would limit himself to a mostly tomato diet. He lost seventy pounds and was at his optimum weight. But how would he maintain this new freedom? How would he continue in his newfound health? He expanded his diet past the tomatoes and the occasional protein he was enjoying. He liked pumpkin and canned pumpkin was cheap. Canned pumpkin, fresh acorn squash, spaghetti squash, squash of any and every kind was his newfound staple. He was satisfied and we rejoiced.

Jim was thin.

Jim was also changing color.

He went away to speak at a men's retreat where it was noted that he was a beautiful shade of orange. Men are not impressed if their speaker glows. Women find it unbelievable that men noticed at all.

So much for that diet.

Jim returned to our life of expressing love through food. He has considered turnips, but they are not as hospitable as pie and coffee.

QUESTIONS FOR REFLECTION:
Why is dependency bad?
Why have food at a ministry at all?
If food is love, how can accountability equal love?
Is a well-ordered ministry good or bad?

When institutional giving no longer meets a need, how do you dissolve the relationship?

What are the first and second steps of help that a church can do?

What consequences are there to hospitality?

CHAPTER 5

GROWING IN
LOVE AND GOOD WORKS

Neighborhood Academy
VBS Comes to the Inner City
Medical Clinic

NEIGHBORHOOD ACADEMY

At times, the needs around us have been so great we've had difficulty seeing them. God has allowed others to see the needs for us.

Joy and Doug, who are now part of our church leadership, had been part of the community for about a year when they first began talking about a school. They were drawn to work in the inner city and we were the only church that didn't make one or the other of them mad.

They had been looking for a church that had both sound theology and practical help for the needy. Doug was in Bible College in those days and people there had heard about our church plant. They came from solid middle-class backgrounds, though Joy's parents and grandparents had been intimately involved in church ministry. So they initially drove in to church. It wasn't long before they moved into the neighborhood.

They were particularly good at seeing needs and getting ministry rolling the right way. From their first connection with the church, both Doug and Joy valued hands-on ministry. They helped when we had to clean houses, pass out food, or care for children. Doug and Joy prodded the church to a greater teaching ministry. As they continued to minister in the community, they felt that we should focus on the need of the teens to be educated. There wasn't one high school student in the entire youth group that expected to graduate from high school.

Joy came to Jim and said, "We could start a school."

Jim immediately responded with, "You're out of your mind. We can't even get this wreck of a building sorted out."

Joy dismissed that comment with a clear statement: "Yes, we could!"

She knew that if we started with just a few students, maybe three or four, and gave them the materials they were ready for, they could succeed. "It would be a lot like home schooling," she said. "We could take a product that was already on the market and adapt it to our church's need."

Our first response was to continue in incredulity, but Joy insisted she knew we could. Joy recruited the first of many volunteers. Linda, Debbie's mother was up for the task as well.

As an important aside, Debbie's mother, Linda, was not just our mother and mother-in-law, she was the mother of the church. The joy of the Lord was Linda's language. She was effervescent for Jesus. Linda's youth had been Indianapolis inner-city poverty. She didn't like the thought of moving back into it at first, but when she and Debbie's dad (Phil) did, they were dynamic.

Linda and Phil were the church leaders who had taught our generation of church leaders how to do ministry. Phil led as the first elder of the church, and Linda was the "yes, we can" of her family and the young families who had banded together to start a new church. Linda cared for every child. We saw her teach the married women of the church how to love their husbands and minister with them. She led difficult, we mean *difficult,* older women to the Lord. She was used of the Lord to have Bible study with the mother and grandmother of two of our adopted children. She encouraged all of us to be faithful. She showed us that humble beginnings were just the kind of preparation that Lord would glory in.

Linda and Phil had ministered in rural communities where churches had failed and needed to start again. Linda couldn't believe that the Lord would call them into the heart of the trouble of the city with us, but she was willing. The city needed her joy. The church needed her to be grandma to all the children. The church leaders needed her example and teaching. We needed her encouragement.

After a year-long illness and hospitalization we couldn't believe that she was gone. That was more than ten years ago and we still tear as we think of how much loss comes from love. Our loss of her affected every relationship we have. It is a deep place in our hearts that allows us to minister to others' losses. It is part of deep waters of mercy that the Lord uses to comfort others.

The school has been going ever since, with an average of fifteen students any given year. We take kids who are in trouble if they are part of our community. And we have added a few stable kids to help live as examples of good behavior. We do our best to build up each young person and our hope is that they will graduate with a diploma.

Getting a diploma is a practical goal that is tied up in our primary goal. We want everyone to follow God. God's commands include His call that we care for our own burdens as well as others. It is nearly impossible to break free of the sinful life that so many of our community's families bear up under, or continue in, if they are never able to get to a position where they have something to share. It's our hope that a diploma will lead to a means of financial support. We are breaking a cycle of foolishness, as well as God's curse on the families of those who hate Him.

In the Ten Commandments passage, God promises to curse the third and fourth generations of those who hate Him. We are seeing people break this curse with Christ, with discipleship, with good decisions, and with a diploma. Our school kids are able to make choices— educational choices, financial choices, work choices and family choices that are not available to others around them. They can now honor Christ with the knowledge and character they have developed.

They are in a position to stay in the community and show others how to live. They are also in a position to change the world even as they have been changed.

Sometimes we can make the excuse that foolishness in the city is tied to broken systems, like bad school systems, bad foster care policies, broken families, the drug life, limited opportunities, and disincentives to work. Joy was one who said, "It will stop here." She put her time, her family, her energy, her friendships, all that she had, at the disposal of those first four children.

One particular young lady is a good example of the educational success that we've had. She was unwilling to go to our local high school. Somehow she wasn't making it and she was unwilling to go any further. We tested her, and she measured third grade in most subjects and kindergarten in one. After a year she was in fifth grade materials in every subject. We couldn't believe the success. What a delight. We would have liked it very much if she moved further along in her walk with the Lord. In fact, that's our first goal; we would rather have people follow God in some depth, than have them graduate with a diploma recognized by the world. But we can't make decisions for people. We strive hard for both educational and spiritual growth.

The school continues because it is more than an educational platform. It is a platform for discipleship. It is an opportunity for ministry. It is a delight to see kids move forward. Some of our stable children have gone on to Bible colleges, some to work as missionaries or social work. Some who have graduated have grown to make good life choices that have included staying connected to God and His people. This makes all of us involved in the school proud. As far as we know, all but one of our students have stayed out of jail, and most have joined society in some productive way.

For these blessings we are thankful.

Debbie is regularly in the school. She takes her turn, a couple times a week. She finds teaching the little ones a pleasant challenge, though tiring. There are one or two of those little ones that make me crazy. However, they've not been taught at home how to listen. How could they learn to follow instructions? These little ones, whose families are touched with mental health issues, drugs, and rebellion, really do appreciate the fact that anyone would care for them, feed them, and love them. They also understand that someone is responsible for them in the church.

Over the years, we have had every kind of volunteer imaginable. Professional teachers as well as professional maintenance men have brought their gifts and care for the children to school. These days we have people with medical degrees, nursing degrees, world travelers, authors, and trained therapists all teaching. We have many from the top of society as well as some who have come through the same troubles these kids have come through. We have individual prayer partners for each child. There has been an outpouring of help from every part of society. People want to help and this institution has allowed many to use their skills and limited time to do something.

Our greatest success may not be with the children; it may actually be with the adult volunteers who have found a way to endure the brokenness of our community, even our century-old building, in order to fulfill God's call to care for others.

Oftentimes, a Christian school will say that they are one of three legs in a three-legged stool. Neighborhood Academy, however, is not one leg but all three. We are a stump. The legs are school, church, and family. The biological family is broken. The public school system is broken. The community is broken. The church, however broken, must love with the power God gives. It must gather around and care for the least of these. We will care for these children, and bring them up as though we are family. And when we are reminded that some of these kids are in real trouble, there are enough of us around to remind the others that the kids are doing so much better than they did last year.

We have great hope at Neighborhood Academy, not only for the educational needs of the kids, but great hope for the spiritual well-being and the rebuilding of what is broken in community.

VBS COMES TO THE INNER CITY

For years, our friend Patty has brought an entire entourage to Neighborhood Fellowship during the summer. She knew that if she could staff a Vacation Bible School that had well-produced materials and drew a good group in the suburbs, they could do VBS in the inner city as well.

All we at Neighborhood Fellowship had to do was bring the children. Initially, there were logistical things to work out, but Patty would not be thwarted. She said if we can do this for Zionsville Fellowship, then we can come downtown and do this for those who have nothing.

The logistical things that needed sorting out included the fact that all of the volunteers helping with VBS were available in the mornings, but all the young people that were part of Neighborhood Fellowship wouldn't normally be up until the afternoon.

As missionaries who have been trained to think about culture, it has been our habit at Neighborhood Fellowship to adapt to the community we work with. And yet we had two cultures to deal with. We don't like it when the more affluent culture is catered to for the sake of giving honor to those who already have everything else. But if we're unwilling to adapt, we couldn't have the workers. Compromise is sometimes God's wisdom. We were giving honor to those who were the workers. If the only time they could come was early, then we would find a way to wake up sleepy kids.

For a dozen years or so, Patty has worked hard to organize and administrate what is hard to organize and administrate. Patty often calls our form of VBS "organized chaos." She has made sure that we start with breakfast and that the volunteers are on time. She has made sure that we have leaders who could lead the singing and that there are enough leaders to handle all the young people. Because relationship is important in our community, the fact that volunteers from Neighborhood Fellowship are picking our kids up and are there throughout the classes all help to make things run smoothly.

We have children who have autism. We have children who have anger control issues. We have children who suffer from oppositional defiance disorder and assorted illnesses. We have other children who have just had a difficult upbringing. These children need special attention, but the suburban volunteers were willing to handle it, because they were warned and we could intervene.

Those volunteers who come downtown give testimony of the blessing that they received. One business owner closes shop and brings his entire office to volunteer. They've seen compassion at work and some of these volunteers themselves have received Christ as their Savior.

One of the cultural values that distinguishes Neighborhood Fellowship from our friends in the suburbs is that we do not use last names. Children, as well as adults, call us and everyone in our church by their first names. Last names are often shaming. Yet the distinction between the cultures could be sorted out because the Neighborhood leaders explained that respect could be shown in other ways. Another way that our friends who come to do VBS accommodated us was by allowing children to group in families when they were accustomed to grouping children by age. Again, this was done to make our children feel at home. Many of their parents would say to the older children, "Don't let the little one out of your sight." So our more affluent friends accommodated our culture even though they would have liked to train us in the "right" ways. They accommodate us and hopefully we do the same.

Another way that our community was different from those who came to serve was seen at dismissal. The bus would pull up, children would be given their sack lunch, and often time adults would gather outside of the building—not because they had children in the building, but because they realized that it might be possible to get a sack lunch. It's not that we live in a particularly greedy community as much as we live in a hungry one. This would never have happened in the more affluent community.

It would've been very easy for our suburban friends to be unbending. They could have said, "No. If you can't meet us on our terms, we are unwilling." But somebody must bend and this is a good secondary step for someone from a suburban situation engaging in ministry in the city.

Vacation Bible School provides an opportunity for children to hear the gospel, have food, love, playtime, and safe people watching after them. VBS is a great kindness to the young people, as well as an encouragement and a blessing. The care continues when children are sent home with sack lunches. Jesus says, "It is more blessed to give than receive" and "let the little ones come unto me."

Each year, after pictures of all the children have been taken, we have a celebration Sunday where the volunteers come and worship with Neighborhood Fellowship. We go out and just enjoy the fact that we are all in Christist. What a beautiful coming together. What an amazing kindness from God. If there is ever a picture of what heaven will be like, we get a glimpse of it on that Sunday.

We're thankful, particularly for Patty. We are also thankful for the many who have come and worked as servant-leaders. There's a long list of people who will receive reward from the Lord for what they have done for the least of these at Neighborhood Fellowship. They come with Patty and they do good work and sacrifice their time for others. We see both givers and receivers blessed by the Lord Himself. God bless us all! And He has.

MEDICAL CLINIC

The medical clinic in Neighborhood Fellowship's building is one of the very best parts of ministry. Mature churches educate and are involved with healing. They begin by preaching the Word, then move to the care of others by enlightening their minds and caring for their bodies.

When our friend Dr. Sevilla called, he said, "Jim, I would like to start a clinic in Neighborhood Fellowship."

"Great!" we said.

"Hold on!" he said. "The clinic needs to be free."

"Yes," we said, "got that!"

Dr. Sevilla went on to say, "The clinic needs to be student led."

We said, "We don't know what that means, but if you send candy stripers with band-aids, we will be better off than we are right now."

Dr. Sevilla said "Hold on! I want the students to meet you (meaning the church)".

"You want us to evangelize the doctors?"

"Exactly!"

This was a type of clinic that we had never before imagined.

We had always imagined a clinic where there would be Christian doctors who, out of their faith, would minister to the needy. We never imagined students who were unsure of their faith, or untrained in the things of God, would be learning from us. This was an opportunity that was unbelievable. We would see the needy cared for and, at the same time, be able to engage with those who were learning medicine and the ethics of medicine. When we originally thought about a clinic, we thought we would work three Christian doctors half to death caring for the poor. Dr. Sevilla had a greater imagination which not only included medical care but engaging on a deeper level where Christianity changes cultures. When Christianity is discussed in the public square, it wins the day. It is the winner because it is rational and loving. "Loving your neighbor as yourself" is one of the primary commands of God that cannot be opposed by rational thought.

Love is an answer in and of itself. We don't have to push, but we are glad to present God's Word.

We don't know what to say about the clinic. It has become such a surprise to us. We built out some space in the building. We moved some rooms. We scooted over so that others could care for people in ways that we weren't able to. This seems to be the most natural fit. This clinic is a place where life and health are spoken of and acted out by those in need and those who want to help. It is where sacred and secular have come together in unity for the benefit of others. The students have been instructed in the beginnings of the art of compassion and the art of honoring human dignity. The clients, who we call friends, are the patients who participate with the students. These friends feel the warmth and understand that this is a place that they can find real help. Some of those who come in need come with mental illness, some come with emotional problems, some have no place but the streets to call their own. Some lack insurance and don't know how they are going to pay for their healthcare. Some are those who have looked to other organizations for help and found there was little help with the exception of directions to the clinic that meets in Neighborhood Fellowship's building.

When we had our first EKG in the church building, we were excited about the advancements in technology, as well as the advancement in the expressions of dignity and respect. These eight years of clinic have gone by in a moment, and they continue to get better. The clinic has expanded from a health fair and now includes Indiana

University School of Medicine, Indiana University School of Law, Indiana University School of Social Work, Indiana University School of Dentistry (where else can you get free dentistry?) and Butler University School of Pharmacy. The University of Indianapolis joined in with their School of Physical Therapy. IU then brought on board their School of Physical Therapy as well as the School of Occupational Therapy. IU School or Ophthalmology has come on board as well as IU School of Public Health and IU School of Nursing. Optometry is soon to come. We no longer talk about being interdisciplinary. The clinic is interprofessional! It is the model for the future and is the largest clinic of its kind. It is well managed and set to expand.

Neighborhood Fellowship and the clinic have been recognized by the city of Indianapolis as well as receiving an award from Indiana University and the Governor's award from our state. We are not opposed to being recognized for the good works being done; it just seems that Dr. Sevilla, the students, and people who helped this outreach go forward would be better recipients of any award than we would. Our part in the clinic, and the many schools it represents, is only one of hospitality, something that Christian folk are expected to be given to.

Collaboration with these universities has been an education for Neighborhood Fellowship. We're a church with very simple faith. We often joke that we are the urban Amish. The Scripture says that we are to love our Lord and to love our neighbors as ourselves. In doing so, we found it necessary to take friends and neighbors who are ill to the hospital. We are no longer an emergency ride to the hospital, but are now able to act as the doctors' deputies. We go around to our neighbors as informal health care workers.

This collaboration has also given us great confidence. We initially wondered how such a little group as ours would avoid feeling swallowed up in relationship with such a large group? The collaboration has allowed us to maintain our identity, while the professional schools have maintained theirs. We can stand, both small and big, caring for the same concerns. This collaboration also has allowed us a sense that the sacred and the secular can work together.

The participation of Indiana University-Purdue University at Indianapolis has contributed to Neighborhood Fellowship's capacity to care for others in a much greater way than we had imagined. Whether it be the medical clinic, the legal clinic, the dental clinic, the pharmacy, help that is afforded through the social workers, therapists, or eye doctors, we see suffering people comforted. And we attempt to bring comfort to the students, many of whom need the Lord to direct them in a path that will lead to a better, healthier, joy-filled life. The clinic addresses some of the most obvious needs in the city. The student and teaching faculty who are part of the clinic are not drafted into the faith conversations that many of the patients are interested in. But the clinics provide a place of dignity, compassion, care, things that places of faith should be known for all around the world.

Our hospitality and the students' work is what is being celebrated here. The students, Dr. Sevilla, the teaching physicians and other are held in high esteem by our neighbors. Neighborhood Fellowship is only doing what should be normal for any church, opening its doors so skilled people can care for others.

Some of us at Neighborhood Fellowship find it ironic that the church might be honored for acting like Christians by a secular institution. This clinic model at

Neighborhood Fellowship is already one of the most inter disciplinary clinic models in the county. It could easily be the premier way that universities provide opportunities for their students to practice the good things they are being taught. Schools will be asking for free space and access to the poor that churches should already have. The question is, will churches be willing and prepared to share their buildings, share their relationships, and share their faith?

QUESTIONS FOR REFLECTION:
Who are the "yes, we can" people in your life?
What are the humble circumstances in your life that God will glory in?
What foolish cycles need to be broken in your community?
How do you adapt to the givers when the receivers are the ones in need?
Does your church building have a place that the sick could be cared for?
How does our culture hide its selfishness or racism?
How can you be truly safe?

CHAPTER 6

LOSING THE PROMISE OF HOPE

When Hope came to us she had been in another foster home in the church. Before that she had gone from house to house. This little one's life was completely unstable. Hope was born addicted to heroin. She spent her first week detoxing at the hospital. She had multiple problems linked to her prenatal addiction. She needed regular medical care and she couldn't sleep on any schedule. She stayed with her mom and grandma who didn't have the abilities to keep her. She was one of five children that her mom couldn't keep. Family members stepped in with the others, but Hope couldn't sleep. A number of possible dads were named. The man who was married to Hope's mother had been locked up and wanted nothing to do with the baby.

In foster care, Hope still couldn't sleep. She had already suffered the ill effects of abandonment. She didn't know how to attach to those who cared for her. And then Hope was placed in a loving family. But that family could not keep her. She couldn't sleep and the mother in the home was pregnant. No one would do well in that situation.

Yet our church had taken Hope in as one of the little ones. She was far more than the "least of these." She had wormed her way into our hearts. She was part of us, part of our community, and part of the church. A number of us were foster parents. We knew we had to decide what seems so obvious to us now. We decided, yes, a baby is part of the church, and we needed to step in and care for her.

Hope came to our house, comprised of two parents and six kids, four biological and two adopted. This might become her permanent home. No dad had come forward or been properly identified. Her mother was unlikely to get things sorted out and her mother's family was out of energy. So we began the hard work of teaching Hope to attach by attaching ourselves to her.

She would wake up angry and anxious. At least, that was our diagnosis. She showed us signs of attachment issues. She pushed away from us when we held her close and yet we were to be her foster parents. She had to eat. She had to sleep. She had to attach. With a lot of work she got better, but she still had trouble sleeping.

We're skilled at developing relationships with children who are broken in this way. We've been trained as therapeutic foster parents. We know how to bring a child close. We know how to develop their interest in us and in others. We are good at reinforcing positive views. There was lots of hair combing and looking in the mirrors, words of affirmation, foods to comfort—all that she needed came from our hands. Along with us, our children, our extended family, and our community embraced her as well. And we all know God's commandment to love sacrificially. After some months of work Hope opened her heart to us. In every way we were mommy and daddy. Yet Hope always had trouble sleeping.

Hope is a delight, joy, and pleasure, a bright-eyed little girl. It's obvious she loved us. And we loved her. In her second year she went to physical therapy, occupational therapy, and speech therapy. There had been internal healing in her body and good news about her long-term medical outlook. But Hope, bright and fun, still wouldn't sleep at night.

A father was found. We were brokenhearted. He stepped up in ways that meet the standards for the courts. He had his issues, mental health issues as well as financial issues, yet he was willing to give his time, money, and attention to Hope for his visits. He wanted her with all his heart. He came to court and pledged to take care of her. Yet he had little visible means of support. He was unable to provide a home for himself, but because of his family's charity he had a bed and a room for Hope. His life was far below our minimum standard for this little girl. Dad seemed to us like someone who would make a good grandfather figure. How could one expect responsible behavior from someone who was supported by his daughter's boyfriend?

The judge began planning on sending her home with her dad. It's never been a competition between us and him. If it had been, we would've won hands down. We took on a social responsibility to care for that lovely little child. We couldn't give her our skills without giving her our hearts. Now, brokenhearted, we returned to our God, and we prayed. He knows what's best. We knew that all along. He knows the outcome before the beginning. God is our only comfort. What are we to do?

We waited out the last of the 90 days in which Hope was to go to her dad. We saw all that was wrong with this plan. Any reasonable person could see the problems. Yet, we want parents to have rights. We want parents to be redeemable. We believe that children are tangible blessings from God Himself to their biological families. Yet if this one wasn't ready to handle the blessing properly, how could we rejoice?

So we were, and still are, brokenhearted. What did we expect? Isn't this the end of caring for somebody else's child and attaching to her? Isn't this the fulfillment of James 2:27: "True religion is to care for orphans and widows in their distress and keep oneself unspotted from the world"? Was she never an orphan?

Our friends in the Lord say that caring for children is always right. Yes, this is good. But in the end, it hurts.

Our children mourn and we have to explain to friends and acquaintances how we are doing. It turns out that we are not doing so well.

We are overwhelmed.

We are sad.

We imagine there will be a time of joy, when we begin to understand God's plan, His work, His will. But for now we sorrow. We know the pit of despair. We also know that we will survive. But who wants to survive? We want God to reach into the situation and make it better. Some who see our hurt have prayed imprecatory prayers against those responsible for Hope leaving our house.

We knew losing Hope was a possibility, in some ways a probability. Each of the families that do foster care and adoption have gone through something similar. Those who have experienced this are the most consoling. You can see a crowd of weepy eyes whenever Hope is mentioned. When we think of the court-ordered train wreck that is her present, as well as her future, we are distressed and see the fraying edges of our faith.

Before she left us, she came home from an extended visit with her dad. She reeked of cigarette smoke. She was weepy. To top it all off, she was feverish. Red in the face, crying. It was just a mild temperature, but there is this continued evidence in our hearts and minds that Dad and his extended family are not prepared to care for a little one.

Reunification is always the great goal and we were expected to risk everything for it—but there was a little girl's life that hung in the balance. This reunification may be a success story to some, but it isn't to us. We've never been able to see Hope as a product. She's the little one we let into our hearts. She needs the best this world has to offer.

Many foster parents would congratulate themselves that they had reached the goal of reunification. We couldn't congratulate ourselves. Reunification meant her destruction.

We continue to cry out to God. Now that Hope isn't keeping us up at night, our prayers are. We ask Him what He's doing. We beg Him to bring healing to us and to her biological family. We see with eyes of flesh. But we long to see with eyes of faith.

We're teaching the story of Abraham and his sacrifice of Isaac to the Sunday school children at church. We wonder if Hebrews 11 counts for us. It says that Abraham believed that God was able to raise Isaac from the dead. Is that figuratively, what we're going through? Or are we the people who suffer loss as we minister for the kingdom? Are we the ones who are emotionally sawn in two because of our faith? Philippians tells us that we are to know God and the power of his resurrection, but also the fellowship of the suffering, that we might attain the resurrection of the dead. These are the emotional throes that we go through as we mourn this process. We are going through this with our other foster-parent friends and family church members who have had foster children sent home. They never saw those children in good health again. These children are still suffering. And they are suffering in ways they weren't while in foster care.

We have considerable experience in our church with foster care. Our experiences include a young lady who became part of the community, was sent home and within six weeks was homeless. She wasn't returned to foster care.

Another set of children suffered severe abuse when they were reunited with parents for just a short time. Others marched on to fend for themselves in utter brokenness. Another ended homeless with his mother. We mourn for the loss. One of our regular comments about foster care is that it is man's sinful way of dealing with man's sinful problem. Yet our hearts are still hopeful because we trust God.

We are extremely blessed people. God answers our prayers. He is our defender. He is even our rear guard. We don't know how to express the fact that we can walk in confidence with Him. He has just been especially good to us and we are thankful. We still wonder if the Lord will bless us with a future relationship with Hope. For the last year we haven't been allowed to see her. All we know to do is walk faithfully in our prayer for her. We praise God that His Word tells us that he steers the hearts of rulers like one steers waters. We do not agree with the judge who sent her to her biological dad, a man who within months went to jail. We have a canal not too far from where we live. It reminds us that waters are steered and that God steers the heart of rulers and judges. It reminds us that if man can change the course of great resources, then God can do much more. We cry out with Job, "the Lord gives and the Lord takes away, blessed be the name of the Lord."

Now we will see if any of us can sleep. May God help us all.

POSTSCRIPT

We know sadness. We don't know it in all of its forms. We have not experienced serious personal illness or injury. We've not known war, famine, or even severe marital strife. But suffering has been part of our life and ministry. It is always near in the work we do. Angst is a constant companion to those we care for. There is a low-grade fever of emotional distress for our community. Broken-heartedness is more routine than the common cold. It is a chronic condition that has its acute flare-ups at all the worst times. When it does, the people of God are the hospital. Those gifted in mercy are the physicians and their tonic the healing waters of mercy.

There are times we think that we could do without so much trouble. But in trouble we express the love of God. We pour out mercy and compassion on the broken-hearted. Mercy is a great comfort to those whom it is poured out on. The gift of mercy is a true gift to mankind, yet its weight is difficult for the one who carries it. Mercy, like the power of the cross, is joy to mankind. It is like forgiveness given by the bloodletting of the cross. For our Savior, the cross was the shame that had to be endured for the later joy that would come. For those who have the gift of mercy, the weight is not nearly what our Lord bore for us. Yet it is a weight. We drop a bucket down the well of our heart into God's waters of mercy. We pull it up hand-over-hand on a twine rope without a wench. Each pull is painful, but we grow used to it. Mercy is good in the moment for everyone—that is, except for the one gifted in mercy. True empathy, that includes God's mercy, brings another's suffering into our mind and heart. We, the mercy givers, become the afflicted in spirit. We bear the weight. We bear the anguish of soul and mind and in that identification with another person's pain, there is healing, relief, and God is there in that moment. We endure because His presence is the thing we long for in the deepest parts of our being. The waters of God's mercy splash on us even as we give it to others.

We comfort ourselves that in the end it works out well for the one gifted in mercy, too. The Sermon on the Mount tells us that "Blessed are the merciful for they will receive mercy." We need mercy. Praise God, we can expect it. In the meantime though, Scripture tells us to comfort others with the comfort we ourselves have received.

QUESTIONS FOR REFLECTION:

Should Christians engage with the foster system?
Is sympathy good enough if empathy hurts that much?
What comfort have you received?

CHAPTER 7

PAIN FROM WITHIN
AND WITHOUT

Yes, the Water is Safe
Contrast in Attitude
A Child Problem?
Gentrification
God is Our Rear Guard

GIVING WITH HUMILITY

We know Christians are difficult, but sometimes they can be painfully difficult.

From time to time, someone will suggest that the poor of the church we are part of come together with affluent folk from other churches. On our best day, we are reticent.

There is an assumption in the evangelical world that more affluent church-goers, having accepted the sound teaching in their churches, can therefore, go among the poor and do good work. This might be true if people had an understanding of the first two or three chapters of the book of James. It might even be true if people just treated others as they wished to be treated. Yet, this has proven untrue at many work projects. We are tempted to believe that the affluent are at times unable to do the good they set out to do. On the other hand, we have had some work project days that have been so remarkably good that we ask about the people's preparation and then befriend that group as dear and lasting friends.

It has been suggested to us over the years that a thankful heart is the normative response when affluent people give of their resources and time. The truth is that we do see the good works of our more affluent brothers and sisters in Christ. We are thankful for their gifts. We would like to help some of them with their attitudes. Without specific training in the Scripture they often are slightly ignorant or slightly arrogant. An attitude of condescension is easily available to those who put a few hours work into our desperate community. God commends them to be cheerful givers.

This was Paul's subject matter in I Corinthians 11: "Their meetings did more harm than good. And that is why some of them slept." The Apostle thought that correction was the order of the day, not glossing over the sin of partiality. He thought warning, rather than praise, for bad participation was the way to true healing and unity. We understand Paul's concern.

One year, a group of well-intentioned middle-class and affluent Christians came to our house to help with a summer children's ministry in our home. These are people we've never seen again. We have always had a vibrant kids' ministry at Neighborhood Fellowship. This event happened when the church was meeting in our home. Since we live in the inner city, first-time visitors can be a little nervous. One such adult helper entered the kitchen and asked if the water was safe to drink.

Now, ours is the same water system that everyone in our county drinks from, so we were taken aback. Was it something about our home? Was it something about our appearance? We were dressed reasonably that day, and Jim may have even combed his hair.

Another time, a church called asking if twenty or so volunteers might have an opportunity to do some work in our church building. This group came from an even more affluent church and community. Even though one of us is particularly administratively challenged, we try to accommodate this kind of good work as it is of some help to Neighborhood Fellowship and of eternal value to the givers. This is a place that both rich and poor can celebrate that we are one in Christ. Unity is one of Jesus' highest values according to John 17 and thus it is also one of ours.

This particular church had spoken to us regarding the failure of urban ministries to adequately prepare for work days and admonished us to be on top of it.

The team showed up. All three of them.

The three who showed up were disappointed at the turnout, as were we, and spoke to us as though it must be our fault.

Nonetheless, they planted flowers and cleaned. When the three left together, one woman had left her keys. We found them and made contact. The lady told a detailed and sad story about her fear of traveling through unfamiliar places. It seemed a great phobia. Our hearts went out to her. We are people given to mercy. We said that Jim would be glad to drop her keys off with her husband.

Then she said, "And we have a BMW. You don't think that it would be wise to drive that down there, do you?"

With insult added to injury, Jim went through the trouble of bringing the keys into a lobby of an international pharmaceutical company where arms of welcome for the delivery service were not open wide. Jim wasn't allowed to leave the keys and was told that our van needed to be moved to the other side of the drive. The security guard then confronted Jim for being too long at the information desk and asked the lady at the desk if everything was "normal." She responded yes, everything was "normal." When Jim finally gave up and was driving away, the husband caught him in the driveway. He said he had heard from his wife that ours was "quite a place." He added with a hint of disdain, "She's a neat freak, you know."

We have had work parties come and bring two-, three- and four-year-olds and let them help paint our walls. We would never dream of turning our toddlers loose with paintbrushes in their church building.

No Christians intend to do harm when they sacrifice their time and money to be involved in ministry to the poor. However, sacrifice without knowledge is not enough. Humility of heart listens to God's command to love our neighbor as ourselves. If we truly desire to live in the unity of Christ and obey His commands to care for the poor, we will begin by dialogue not assumption. Just as the poor among the rich would not assume they know which fork to use at dinner, the affluent of this world should not assume that they understand intricacies of the poor. We must all realize that if we meet any Christians, they are our brothers. They need the same respect that we hope to be granted.

CONTRAST IN ATTITUDE

In the last few years, we have had a new set of volunteers coming through to minister with Neighborhood Fellowship. Bernie has been the most excited. He has played keyboard while our adopted son Jacob played the drums at men's retreat. He was amazed at Jacob's natural talent, as are we. We know it came from his biological family. Bernie found out that Jacob played and that our adopted daughter Michelle wanted to cut hair for a living after she graduated high school.

Bernie has a daughter who is a physician. He also has a daughter who is working in hair care. The funny thing is that Bernie is able to do both. He is a nurse as well as someone who cuts hair. He and his family have embraced Neighborhood Fellowship as their newfound favorite place of service. Bernie and his family serve in the clinic, give free haircuts to men and women, wash dishes and much more. What an exciting thing.

Bernie's exuberance is like so many people who perceive the workings of inner city ministry and misinterpret our relational style of embracing poverty as unintentional or an unorganized mess. It is never unintentional. It is only sometimes unorganized. So Bernie looked at the food that was being cooked and said this is too low of a standard. Without telling us, he went out into the community to talk to some folks he knows in the restaurant business. He wanted to see if they would donate meals to our school.

What an exciting thing—Bernie understood that if something needed help or change, that it wasn't his job to organize us, but maybe he could be the means to that change. He would work harder.

This is a great difference between Bernie and many other volunteers who come to Neighborhood Fellowship. We have had many people come and tell us how we could do it better. But the end result of their administration, if we were to follow it, would be that we work harder. Bernie is not such an advisor. He is a doer.

So without talking to us, a momentary awkwardness (what relationship doesn't begin with awkwardness?), Bernie talked to the owner of a restaurant and told him about the food needs for Neighborhood Academy.

The problem is that our food needs were already being taken care of by another institution, one that's highly organized, one that is completely and utterly faithful. It is true, there was room for improvement. Sometimes that highly organized, highly faithful, not-for-profit group would serve food that the children were unwilling to eat. And Bernie had seen some of that. Bernie had also seen this institution in an awkward moment when they were changing out their kitchen. They had counted on us to add our skill and labor and, occasionally, our own food to the mix. We didn't complain and Bernie had no way of knowing this was a temporary arrangement.

Bernie organized food for eighteen students, but we generally serve twenty-five. We don't know the character of the man providing the food. We don't know the longevity of his commitment. After Bernie's exuberance had calmed down a little, we were able to talk through the implications of his help. It seemed like we could work things out, but we needed to ask a few questions.

Bernie and his initial relationships had missteps. But that didn't mean we couldn't get along. And his misstep was a misstep due to his exuberance, his excitement about serving the Lord. We could correct some of the details because the right heart was there, a servant's heart. Bernie has come to the clinic to cut hair and he has gotten the food that was pledged for the school. Instead of burdening us, he has brought a heart of service to add to our ministry. He is strengthening our arm. He moved from one of the volunteers to one of the proactive workers. We have prayed for God to bless him. Now, he continues to add strength to our weakness. We rejoice in our friendship.

Another volunteer at the clinic, a young man that we don't know well) (but we didn't know Bernie that well to begin with either) came to the clinic because he was a friend of somebody who is important at another church. He didn't mind mentioning that he was a friend of that person. Soon after he arrived, he began making statements about how ministry should or should not be done. He did not mind speaking about ministry to other cultures and how Americans can do it best, a subject that does not go over well in our international outreach and community.

This young man was an equal opportunity offender. He insulted those who were Christians and insulted those who were not. He insulted Americans. He insulted international volunteers who had come to help care for the poor. This young man had opinions and was willing to lead in a place where he'd never set foot before.

There is a cultural value among the affluent that teaches young people to lead. Leadership is highly prized among the people this young man comes from, but his form of leadership is at odds, or was at least initially, with the commands of Jesus. Jesus told his disciples that the greatest among them would be the servant of all. There is a servant-leadership that we believe the Lord demands.

At Neighborhood Fellowship, this young man was violating the servant -leadership principle, and violating it hard. He was corrected and he could not hear it because he was corrected by someone "less important" than himself. As he continued in his behavior, he was corrected again and in a much clearer way. He no longer fellowships with us in the work.

The one thing that we have demanded of those who volunteer at the clinic is that they treat people with dignity. They must understand that people are made in the image of God, and although the image of God may be marred in an individual, it is in fact marred in all of us. We treat people with the dignity that we would treat our Maker. We have demanded that Muslim, Hindu, Atheist, Christian and anyone else who comes in our door to volunteer be kind.

First of all, this young man forgot kindness because he was too busy wanting to lead. For some reason he thought that his connection to Neighborhood Fellowship and those that are important in churches that relate to us, was enough to make him important. Unlike Bernie, this young man did not know what being a servant is.

Hopefully this is a misstep. Missteps happen all the time, to the best of us, with the best intentions. We love to tell stories of how we made missteps in our ministry. It reminds us that God is the one who does great things and that we're just His instruments. The one thing that we do not bear well is arrogance. Pride is the very thing that destroyed God's most beautiful angel. It's the thing that God detests. It's the thing that makes us fall. So this young man, hopefully, simply missed the mark in those first moments. We hope that he will hear God who is opposed to the proud, but gives grace to the humble. If this young man responds positively, we will have another brother come back to the work. If he never gets the right attitude, he will remain outside ministry with us. In the meantime we have prayed for God to help him.

A CHILD PROBLEM?

It has been confirmed by yet another suburban church goer that our church has "a real child problem." The first time we heard it we couldn't believe it actually came out of someone's mouth. The one who said it immediately corrected himself by saying "I mean there sure are a lot of children here."

There sure *are* a lot of children coming to our inner-city church. "Child problem" is not how we have described our condition. We are glad to care for the large number of children that a young congregation has, but we are even more pleased to obey God's regular command to care for the fatherless. If one thought that children could ever be a problem, we would have to confess that we are not only full, we are infested. It seems that other churches must have called for exterminators, but we don't have a heart for that. We don't know where the child catcher from Chitty Chitty Bang Bang lives. The fact is that we are happy with having as many children as God will allow us to care for. We see children as cute, thus we keep feeding them. We seem to have some in the congregation who keep bringing them to church. They think that church might be good for the children. Some have the audacity to think that children might even be good for church.

And yet once again, we were told that we had a real child problem by one of our visitors from the suburbs. We laughed when we discussed how she went about it. She wanted to know if we had a bus program. We don't. Families bring their children and others from around the neighborhood. Our service must have seemed unruly. It didn't seem so to us. It started with the regular rush to the seats when the first two songs are sung. It may have seemed unruly when we dismissed kids from the service to go to Sunday School. Whatever the trigger was, our children seemed too much or too many.

Unlike the many churches in our inner-city neighborhood that have no children, we have an abundance. And we have a future. Many of the most ornate buildings around us have only a handful of elderly people left. Other congregations are unwilling to have the mess, confusion, or fuss that encouraging these children into their buildings brings. They talk about how children are no longer raised to appreciate the things of God. They might even say that they wish they were in a position to help those who are brought up as rebellious or worse, without any Christian knowledge.

These aging congregations forget the Lord's last command to the church to go into all the world and make disciples. They glory in the accomplishments of the past rather than obey God in the present. They make excuses about their age or weakness rather than seeing these things as encouragements to get busy before they see their Maker face to face. These groups become former churches meeting in buildings, not living, vibrant churches the gates of Hell will not prevail against. Their buildings become tombstones or monuments reflecting the past rather than lighthouses of the present. Worse, these so called churches with their buildings could become incubators for the future, yet somehow they keep the children out.

We have heard the sayings, "If you can't feed them don't breed them." Or, "Poor folk have poor ways." And, "Now that they have their girl or boy maybe they can stop."

These sayings are born of a frustration with a broken society that will have nothing to do with the children. Children are a blessing from the Lord. When was the last time people in any church prayed and didn't ask for blessing for themselves? We, an inner-city church, are proud to scoop up as many blessings as will fit in our building. When one understands the Scripture, he can agree with Jesus who said let the little children come unto Me for such is the kingdom of heaven. As one understands the Scripture he also knows that it would be better for a millstone to be hung around our necks than to offend one of these little ones.

We had our first neighborhood parade with a tractor and everything. We had some of our kids participate and they had a great time. Next year we hope to have a church section with stroller after stroller and a long banner that says, "Our church has a future, come join us." It is true— we have a real future and the children are God's blessing.

GENTRIFICATION

Our neighborhood is being gentrified. City officials have chosen to give us a facelift and we don't like it. Federal money is now available for the redevelopment of our ten streets. Our former neighbors could not stay. Yes, their houses were wrecks, below community standards, but that has been the case for the eighteen years we have lived here. Yet the health department has brought its laser-beam focus to our community.

The difficulty is that the demand for change has come all at once. This demand for improvement, without help to improve, means that some of our neighbors can't stay. In politics, we call this an unfunded mandate. They, nor their landlords, could do the work necessary to bring the individual properties up to standard. So people who had little resources began to move away. Even though we moved to this neighborhood to intentionally identify with the poor for the sake of the Gospel, we knew the day was coming when some would leave. So many have left that we don't recognize our community any more. So many have left that we don't have the sense of community that we once had. Our neighborhood has become like an empty sea shell waiting for a new occupant. The seven once full but now empty houses surrounding ours are a testimony to the change.

We first heard this term gentrification over twenty-five years ago in Chicago. The Uptown neighborhood was going through a dramatic change. Run-down apartment buildings were being reclaimed. People with resources were moving in and changing things. Dilapidation was being replaced by renovation. Slums were now condos. Crime was down in Uptown. New stores were springing up. All was getting better.

Or was it? The property was getting better. The tax base was getting stronger. The specific people who had been there were clearly replaceable. One by one, family by family, residents of that "hood" were threatened with fines, and insurmountable red tape.

Our view about the present predicament comes with years of watching communities change. In the last gentrification of parts of our city, the unwelcome poor were paid what the market would bear for run-down properties. They were sent on their way with additional benefit of moving expenses. Everyone congratulated themselves on a job well done. The poor left with something and the developers had been "generous." After all, they could have just had the city impose eminent domain, but that would have ended with a fight. Developers had their way with cash and it was declared a win-win situation. Well, for everyone except those whose neighborhoods the poor moved into. Neighborhoods that had once been well maintained now had new ill-equipped neighbors.

The plight of the poor was not improved. In fact, they were now further away from the supporting social network that once helped them. Often those who need a hand up are only given a handout. "Give a man a fish or teach a man to fish?" What happened here was that the poor were taken somewhere else to fish.

Our extended family has five generations of experience living in our city. We "remember when" all too often for the comfort of those around us. History has its place in our home. It is exalted next to the study of the Scripture and our care for the poor. This has allowed us to see trends of convection and abuse. A new area will be built well, with craftsmanship and good materials, and all will rejoice. We can see its place in the city as another piece of fine jewelry added to a much-loved collection. The new stone condos downtown and some of the city's gated communities are being built with old-world craftsmanship. These living spaces will be cherished for generations. They will naturally go through their fifty- to seventy-year convection cycle. They will be kept up for a few generations and then they too will fall to the poor. But many of these homes will be able to be lifted up again because of the materials and workmanship. These homes act as the city's backbone. They become a place of lasting endurance that reflects a wise past and a beautiful future. Many of these developments begin with growing pains though. Just as there is a flashiness about new wealth as opposed to an understated allegiance to old money, the same is true with fine new construction. New residences wanting the attention that new opulence brings often misjudge the permanency of public opinion about a new address.

Other areas, like the vinyl-clad houses just inside our interstate circle, have been built up with poor quality material and shoddy workmanship. We mourn how short the life cycle is for these homes. In less than twenty years many of these have already become the slums. Others are waiting just a few more years before becoming tomorrow's slums. In any case, all buildings seem to have their predictable life cycle. Some endure long enough to carry the city into a positive future, and some are like trendy outfits or like stylish haircuts, attractive now but unwanted next season. The poor of Indianapolis are now moving to those vinyl homes.

Gentrification's weakness is its lack of imagination. Those who want the beauty, convenience, nostalgia, or pride of place that comes from being in an area that is transitioning from poor to affluent, do not value what God considers valuable, the people who already live there. They want what they want for themselves. They diminish the beauty, character, intelligence, and tenacity of those who have hung on through the trouble. They also diminish the reflection of God in the individuals who are being displaced. Gentrification is often seen as a rescue mission for the property. But at what time did our nation, let alone those who know God, give up on caring for people?

We cannot ignore that displacing the poor to benefit the wealthy goes against all God teaches us about humility. In the Scripture, the poor have an exalted place in God's family. According to James, they are rich in faith and they should glory in their high estate. We have counted ourselves as the poor since we began ministering in a particularly blighted part of Indianapolis. But because the poor and the foolish are gathered together in blighted neighborhoods, for the last fifteen years we have endured regular gunfire in the alleys and the streets. We know many of the neighborhood prostitutes by name. We have seen the inhumanity of groups of young men gathering together to win the minor street wars that leave many bloody and set these young men on a course of life in prison.

Of all people, we desire to see our neighborhood amenities improve and our property prices go up. Yet our first concern is for people. The foolish should be warned, and may God help the places they are displaced to.

Until we come up with a better plan like moving more affluent people among the poor, this destructive form of gentrification will continue just like that old Pete Seeger song, "Where have all the flowers gone?" For those who are too young, its chorus includes, "When will they ever learn? When will they ever learn?" Convection over stability will be the norm. Places and property will be valued over people. The poor will keep moving. And those poor people will be headed to a poorly built community, possibly near you.

GOD IS OUR REAR GUARD

Neighborhood Fellowship had been in its rundown church building for three years when we first understood institutional oppression. We were overwhelmed with the needs of our community, and now, on top of those needs, we had a wreck of a building.

When we first began the process of buying the building, some of us were shouting how glorious this amount of space could be while others of us walked with our heads hung low seeing the work that was ahead. We could go to the basement and look through the ceiling and through the main floor to the next ceiling to the top floor and through that ceiling. From the basement, you could look up and see daylight.

Yet the church building is where we saw that promise of Isaiah about being rebuilders of walls most readily played out. These old church buildings in the inner city are built for what churches do. They make wonderful platforms for ministry. We had already had the experience of ministry out of our home. That was both glorious and exhausting, but we kept growing and needed more space. We moved to a storefront where we were able to do more of what the Lord had told us to do, preaching the gospel, baptizing, and teaching people to observe all things He had commanded. Now, our group had reached over sixty people, and for special events one hundred and we didn't fit in the storefront anymore. What were we to do?

A church building nearby was available and we rejoiced to have all the space. More space truly equals more people. Although more people in poverty does not mean more resource. It equals more need.

The auditorium of this building had all the stained glass in place, though the plaster was falling off the walls in large chunks and a steady rain of dust fell from the ceilings. That section of the building was almost 100 years old. The education building, with its three floors was 72 years old; its roof leaked like a sieve.

The original workman missed building a supporting wall on the I-beam construction by about a foot and a half. This meant that the roof became a funnel and the water damage would continue until we propped up the roof, rebuilt some walls, and then put a new roof on. There was work to be done all the time. We and our friends were not afraid of work. We worked a little bit here, a little bit there, preaching, teaching, caring for the needs of other, and on the side we would work on the building. Whatever group that might come to visit us and volunteer, would be directed to the physical structure. Whatever spare time anyone had could be swallowed up by this physical need.

Our church building has pretty stained glass, but it is a place where the people are holy, not the bricks and the glass. Having said that, we do like the building, and we find it useful for ministry. After three years of ministry in the building, our family went on vacation with another missionary family, friends who were ministering in British Columbia. We met halfway and took the opportunity to camp in Yellowstone. We showed up in August and it was snowing. We have some amazing memories of the trip, the dust storm that tore RVs apart in Wall, South Dakota, and the fact that our car made it back. But while we were resting, Satan was busy. The church was coming under attack, and under attack from every area.

The most significant was that the public school system had decided to tear down its oldest building and build a new building. The plans for the new building included tearing down **our** church building. Even though we had been working, the church still looked like a beat-up, worn-out, old German church building. There was plenty of busyness connected to the ministry, lots of people, but nothing those who see improvements in property, rather than improvements in people, wanted.

The community desired a prominent new school. It would be an anchor for the start of rebuilding in our area. A new school building was so desired that the threat of eminent domain toward the church seemed acceptable to those who otherwise seemed reasonable. The first thing we ever heard about this possibility came while we were away, and the other leaders of the church were dealing with it in our absence. They were overwhelmed. They were angry. They were frustrated. And when we got the information we, too, were overwhelmed, angry, and frustrated. We gathered together all our relationships who understood real estate law, to discuss what should be done. Some saw this as an opportunity for us to gain some money and be able to have a newer, more suitable building. Others saw it as an attack on the church. No one believed that there was any way we could prevail against eminent domain. We were paralyzed by the power of the state. How could we, simple people, sort this out? All we could do was pray.

The elders at Neighborhood Fellowship agreed that we would do what Romans said, "Bless those who curse you, bless and curse not." We would not say a word against our new antagonists. They were not the problem anyway. We understood that we wrestle not with flesh and blood but principalities, powers, and rulers of this dark age. We would pray. And if any one asked, we would explain our plight.

The media and Christian lawyers were being recruited by some of our more affluent friends. One group, the Alliance Defense Fund, eventually heard of our trouble and came to our aid. They said Indiana's constitution was like that in sixteen other states where there is the question of which laws trump other laws. The question was, do religious liberties supersede state property rights, or do state property rights supersede religious liberties?

Some came to our leadership and said you cannot win against eminent domain. This fight was not ours. We were along for the ride, but the Lord Himself had to work out a plan. We asked the Lord that we be able to stay and yet we were willing to go.

We explained to the public school system that when we had moved the church three quarters of a mile from our house to the storefront, half of our congregation was unable to walk the extra distance, so we were unwilling to move any more than a mile from our present location in the future. The school system dismissed our need. They didn't consider us part of the community. We lived there, but we were of little importance in their minds. What is a church when it stands in the way of progress? They had a thirteen-million-dollar building to build. They weren't about to let a 100-year-old rundown church building and a few poor people stand in their way. Yet our little group, with God's help, was a mighty army of prayer. We asked the Lord to defend us. Then other Christians got the news and came from every direction. They wanted to see the David and Goliath story one more time. Christian lawyers joined forces to come to our aid, even though we had no resource to pay them. The first group to offer money was the Alliance Defense Fund itself. Tens of thousands of dollars were available for lawyers' fees. The first check came and more was pledged. The public school system realized that this would be a long battle in the Indiana Supreme Court and maybe even further. The elders were never happy that this battle had come to them; they just wanted to continue the work of ministry. Yet we praised God that He let us see His glory in this.

In the end, the public school system built their building directly behind our church building, leaving our church building and parsonage fully intact. Before the building began, those representing the school system came to us and said that they wanted to be a good neighbor. They asked if we would like parking.

All we could say was "go away." They'd already handicapped us for six months. They'd gone after us in every way possible. We wanted nothing to do with them.

The representative of the public schools came around a second time and said that they wanted to be a good neighbor and again asked if we would like parking. And again, we responded that we didn't think them trustworthy, that they had done everything to harm us.

A third time they came to us, and we said "Yes. Thank you." We now have rights to parking, eight spaces every day and all the parking Wednesday nights and Sundays. We don't need it so much on Wednesday night, but it is convenient on Sunday.

God delivered us just as He promised. He was our rear guard. He protected us in every way. He sent us just the right people at just the right time. Those people who stood as our adversaries, who were dismissing us, thought that they were just bending down to pick a worm up and throw it out of the way. What they mistook as nothing turned out to be precious to the Lord. God turned to give them attention they didn't want. In the end, He allowed them to build a nice school for the community and parking for us.

QUESTIONS FOR REFLECTION:

Who are work projects supposed to benefit?
Who should organize work projects?
How will you avoid assumption?
How do you recover from pride?
How do you see children in the church?
How do you tell the difference between the poor and the fools?
How has God defended you?

CHAPTER 8

98 PROVERBS OR SHORT SAYINGS AT THE STRIETELMEIER HOUSE

Few of these sayings, proverbs or observations are unique to the Strietelmeier household. This list is meant to give you insight into a family that is trying to live a godly life in a needy community. It also should stand as an encouragement and an example to you and your family as you record your own family sayings. Hopefully all of our sayings will become those that are pleasing to the Lord.

Live like you're camping. Camp like you're stranded.
Life Experience

We have learned to live with brokenness.
Life Experience

Treat older men as fathers and older women as mothers.
Scripture

We'll see if it makes it.
Life Experience

Wisdom is known by her children.
Scripture

Adoption is what God and his people do.
Applied Scripture

Girls, don't bring him home unless he owns a plaid shirt.
Ornamental boys list

We are the urban Amish.
Mission strategy

We are technologically advanced to 1927.
Life Experience

Blessed are the merciful.
Scripture

We don't minister to the poor. We are the poor.
Mission strategy

We are called to be faithful.
Applied Scripture

Not going to get bit by that dog twice.
Hillbilly Roots

There are 10 categories of people that God is particularly concerned with: the hungry, the homeless, the naked, your own flesh and blood, the thirsty, the sick, the prisoner, the stranger, the orphan, the widow, the brokenhearted
Applied Scripture

We trust in the name of the Lord our God.
Scripture

You got to mess up in order to clean up.
Hillbilly Roots

Judas was interested in stewardship also.
Applied Scripture

Eat the best food first, then you are always eating the best.
Hillbilly Roots

Yes. We always do get lost in the worst parts of town.
Life Experience

Rule No. 1: Always take your own car.
Life Experience

If it ain't broke, don't fix it.
Hillbilly Roots

If it gets down into the 70's at night, we can live through the heat.
Life Experience

It's one thing to suffer for righteousness, it's another thing to suffer because of stupidity.
Applied Scripture

Bad art is better than no art.
Mission strategy

Go ahead, swing!
Life Experience

A bird in the hand is worth two in the bush.
Americanism

You got to prime that pump.
Americanism

I love you, but I hate your stuff.
Life Experience

The meek will inherit the earth. Literally!
Scripture

What comes around goes around. You do reap what
you sow.
Applied Scripture

Above all, the servant of the Lord must be gentle.
Applied Scripture

God means it for good.
Scripture

Step away. Give a little time to see what God is doing.
Life Experience

God is not the only one who can give you a raise. Satan
knows how to distract with money.
Life Experience

Too much pumpkin will make you orange.
Life Experience

There are only two commandments and one commission.
Applied Scripture

There is a minimum standard for biblical literacy.
Life Experience

The car was stolen again.
Life Experience

The kingdom is being taken by forceful men.
Scripture

The health department is the new police force.
Life Experience

Slow gentrification gives the poor a chance.
Mission strategy

Don't you know that God has chosen the poor of this world to be rich in faith? *Scripture*

Our retirement plan is sitting around the table.
Life Experience

There are light green people and there are dark green people.
Life Experience

We have an eternal retirement plan.
Applied Scripture

Bless those who curse you, bless and curse not.
Scripture

Yes we can.
Mission strategy

Everyone is expected to share.
Applied Scripture

The sufferings of this world are not worthy to be compared to the glories of the one to come.
Scripture

We tried to keep the insanity outside the house.
Mission strategy

Chocolate is not the answer to everything.
Life Experience

He got MRSA again?
Life Experience

He has a career in radio ahead of him.
Parenting

Which would you rather have—a three-year-old building or a 300-year-old building? *Mission Strategy*

We have effectively become part of the lunatic fringe.
Life Experience

We need a passport to get north of 86th St.
Life Experience

Then came the vermin. Rats. Lice. Mice.
Life Experience

I prefer funerals to weddings. You know how things are going to work out.
Applied Scripture

If you abide in Me, and My word abides in you, ask what you wish and it will be done.
Scripture

Seek first the kingdom of God and His righteousness and all these things will be added to you.
Scripture

Faith comes by hearing and hearing by the word of God.
Scripture

Study to show yourself approved, a workman that needs not to be ashamed, rightly dividing the word of truth.
Scripture

A little slumber, a little sleep, a little folding of the hands to rest...
Scripture

An unenforced law is no law at all.
Philosophy

The unexamined life is not worth living
Philosophy

Squez is the pluperfect of squeeze.
Hillbilly Roots

You will raise up the age-old foundations.
Scripture

And when you call, I will answer.
Scripture

They don't seem to be learning by example.
Life Experience

Care for the hungry, naked, stranger in the land, and don't turn away from your own flesh and blood.
Scripture

Bear your own burdens and bear one another's burdens.
Scripture

It is more blessed to give than receive.
Scripture

We are the most competitive people we know.
Eternal Reward

We are called to incarnational ministry.
Mission Strategy

The greatest among you will be the servant of all.
Scripture

You got the cart before the horse.
Americanism

Money is the answer to all things. *(heavy sarcasm)*
Scripture

If you've done it to the least of these, you've done it unto me.
Scripture

Poor folk have poor ways.
Hillbilly Roots

One boy is a boy. Two boys are half a boy. And three boys
are no boy at all.
Hillbilly Roots

A mist in the pulpit is a fog in the pews.
Old Preacher Saying

Humble yourself under the mighty hand of God and He
will exalt you.
Scripture

The most loving thing she said was, "and you're fat, too."
Life Experience

Blessed are the merciful—they will receive mercy.
Scripture

I check my e-mail once a month, whether I need to or not.
Life Experience

We have a high value on a work ethic.
Mission strategy

The gift of administration doesn't live here.
Life Experience

We were created in Christ Jesus unto good works, which
He ordained that we should walk in.
Scripture

You have been counted worthy to suffer.
Scripture

We wrestle not with flesh and blood.
Scripture

The poor you will have with you always, therefore be generous.
Scripture

Rejoice with those who rejoice, and weep with those who weep.
Scripture

Be all things to all men that you might win some.
Scripture

I couldn't organize myself out of a paper bag.
Life Experience

Somebody isn't loving their neighbor as themselves.
Applied Scripture

I go to the zoo and wonder what they all taste like.
Life Experience

Bless his heart.
Hillbilly Roots

Good!
Life Experience

QUESTIONS FOR REFLECTION:

What are your favorite verses?
Do you have sayings about your ministry?
What proverbs do you teach others?

CHAPTER 9

THE TRUTH OF THE MATTER

South African Train Ride
Cocooned by Danger, Given to Hospitality
Kind Friends the Reward for Helping Others
31 Ideas on Where to Begin
The Transgenders We Have Known and Loved
Faithful Until the End

SOUTH AFRICAN TRAIN RIDE

Time in South Africa was prep for inner-city ministry. We learned that ministry often means upsetting the norm. Sometimes the norm you upset may even be a norm those you are trying to minister to have grown comfortable with. But when upsetting the accepted is the right thing to do you persist, no matter the outcome or the obstacles. Risk everything if you believe it is right. Life and limb. And then when you make a mess of it, try again.

Jim was twenty years old when he went to South Africa and wanted to make a great difference in the country that the world had turned its eyes toward. Apartheid was in place and racism was raging, but not for our generation of Americans. We were the ones who had lived and even thrived in forced integration. We had friends of all races,

118

though in those days we were not very skilled in crossing the cultural divides.

Jim was allowed to live in an Indian township surrounded by a much larger Zulu community. Our desire for church planting would be sharpened as he learned how to navigate the strata of class, race, and religion, including Hindu, Muslim, Animist, and Christian, both nominal and committed. Africa opened Jim's eyes to what identifying with the poor really meant.

This taste of Africa both endeared him to those who lived there as well as helped set the course for our ministry. We would always seek out the poor and be a bridge between cultures. Jim was frustrated that Christians from each ethnic group had believed the lie of apartheid. People were afraid of each other. Even Christians were afraid of other Christians. In their hearts, each group thought that race was their first loyalty. They couldn't imagine a multicultural church no matter how often they read the book of Revelation where it says every tongue, tribe, and nation, will be before the throne of God.

In many ways, the first summer Jim spent in South Africa was a place he would learn what it was to be a minority. He was a minority living among a minority among an oppressed majority. It is one of the few places that he has wished his skin color would change like a chameleon. Having the skin color of the minority oppressors weighed heavily on him.

As he was leaving the country and was alone for one of the first times that summer, Jim decided to identify with the oppressed.

He got to Johannesburg and had to transfer trains. The train platforms were swarming with people and he had to get on the train going to the right destination. He could see that each train had a section marked as white only or for non-whites. Jim is more of a pink-white than any other color. His hair was reddish brown in those days and he could be mistaken as German, but not Zulu. He headed down the platform toward the non-white section hoping no one would stop him. He hung around there for the twenty minutes it took the train to come. There the engine pulled in and the first cars had BLANC printed in large letters. Those passed and then came the unmarked cars for non-white travelers.

Jim saw three black men get in the next car. Jim followed, getting on at the back door. The three African men assumed that Jim was claiming the car as a white car and would start trouble, so they immediately got off. Further oppressing the people he hoped to identify with was not the plan, but it was the result. Jim would not be deterred or left alone. He ran back to the next car where it was already mostly full and there wasn't enough time for anyone to get off. He asked to sit by a large African man who had dressed for Johannesburg's cooler weather. He had a felt hat and his knob-carry, an African walking stick/weapon. The train car was deathly quiet for the next fifteen minutes. Not a sound.

The large man asked what Jim was doing there. He said that he was an American and a missionary and thought that this kind of division between people was wrong. As he was talking a tiny, elderly woman ran from her seat to Jim screaming and gesturing. The entire car turned to the commotion. Many rose to their knees on their seats; the screaming and waving continued. Jim thought he was about to die and said all he spoke was English. The elderly lady switched from her African language to English and said that she was so thankful he was there and may God bless him. The train car erupted in joyous conversation and Jim was still alive.

Our work has since then has been marked with the laughter that trying and making a mess should bring. Our work always identifies with the poor. But most of all it is bathed in the desire to take risks for the kingdom of heaven.

COCOONED BY DANGER, GIVEN TO HOSPITALITY

Because of our ministry in the inner city, our children are well aware of the dangers of the world. They not only know how to "just say no," they know those who say yes, and the consequences they live with. They know them in their impaired state. They know them after the permanent damage. Our children know the names of those who face the horror of lives spun out of control with drugs, theft, mental illness, and loss. They know the names of the prostitutes on Tenth Street. They have held babies suffering from their mothers' drug addictions. Our children's childhood has been invaded by the awareness of dangers of all kinds.

Our house has been broken into. One night we were awakened from sleep to find the intruder just inches away. We have lost possessions, including our vehicles which have been stolen multiple times. Our kids have been in the middle of the storm of danger. A stray handgun was found in our yard, and multiple cars have burned in our alley.

The police have often been on our block with guns drawn. Our children's friends have been both victims and perpetrators of some of the worst crimes in our city. Our children have a skewed view of the country we live in. But their view of faith is clear. You either belong to God or you don't. If you belong to God, than you live like it. And though one might stumble in their walk with God, if they know God, their life is still marked by a growing Christ-likeness.

We have always expected that there would be hypocrisy among the criminals that live in the city. To pass yourself off as the noble poor, or the godly poor, is a liar's means to the next handout. The joy that we find in the search for truth is a reassurance that we are actually doing good. It is the work of those who are gentle as doves and as wise as serpents.

The demand of the truth helps us to find those who are in need (some through no fault of their own), and empowers the urban Christian giver to great sacrifice. The search for the truth is not a witch hunt; it is an invitation to the very presence of Christ, who is the truth. The truth helps us find who needs help and who needs to change. The needy person has needs met and the liar is found out through this sifting of stories and culling truth from half-truth.

One of our favorite liars visited us fifteen times. We made no impression on his memory but each and every time he used a variation of the same outlandish story. We learned to enjoy the diversion as entertainment. In the end, he confessed that he was a pathological liar and we didn't see him again. But when we find one who is not scamming us and our community, we are glad to give.

One of the most difficult things to explain to our children is how those outside the trouble of the inner city call themselves Christians when they act without a high respect for God. We have had the misfortune of meeting with youth groups, Bible school students and respected adult leaders who have not met the basic standards of common courtesy, let alone Christian dignity.

In a suburban situation, without the violence, without the grinding poverty, it seems that a walk with God would be easier, free from the distractions of trouble. Yet we have observed some behaving one way in front of their own congregations, but another way in front of the poor. Some attend church weekly, they invest time and money to be in good standing with a local body, but when they are with those they believe do not matter, their behavior, language, and promises do not seem to matter.

In our community, since honesty is our friend, we can just say that a person is or isn't a Christian based on their behavior. We are not judging their worth. We don't have special glasses that can see God's Spirit. We might be occasionally wrong, but fortunately, for us, we don't have to lie.

The politeness of the majority Christian culture misidentifies people willingly. Many people in society are considered good for the simple lack of criminal evidence against them. However, Jesus says there is none good but God. We look for the goodness of God in someone's life before we are willing to label them one of God's children. The pretense of goodness without God is the most destructive illusion possible. It condemns the practitioner to hypocrisy and keeps them from salvation. It isn't enough to simply associate with God's people; God must be living in the people and through the people. The Scriptures say you will know them by their love for one another. It also says that those who are saved by the Spirit will walk by the Spirit.

We love our local church. We love the Church universal, but we often have to check our attitude toward the larger American expression of the church. It may be that our view is skewed. But as we apply brutal honesty to our own culture, love demands that we are also honest toward those outside the problems of the city. The expectations that we place on our suburban friends seem natural to us. Live life honestly, because only those who walk in the flesh want to be seen as better than they are. Only those at enmity with the Spirit lie. Only the ungodly want to be seen disrespecting God's commands. Only those who have committed themselves to destruction through self-absorption avoid generosity. It seems our inner-city standards are often too imposing for what we have seen of the larger American church. Love demands that we say something.

The area we are most surprised at is the lack of sharing in the dominant Christian culture. This seems to us to be a clear lack of love for one another. Many open their homes to entertaining friends. Some share meals with those they like. But the Scriptures tell us in I Timothy that elders in the church should be "given to hospitality." Most people understand that the phrase "given to drunkenness" comes with a certain habitual nature. So, too, "given to hospitality" must come with a habitual nature. Hospitality is the Greek word that means love of strangers. In a loving, obedient church every opportunity would be sought to spend time with strangers. We cannot count the number of people who have stayed with the leaders of our inner-city church over these past twenty years. All our leaders have had extra people who needed care living with them. Most have taken in foster children.

Most have adopted.

Many have allowed those training for ministry to stay with them for months. Some have kept the physically and mentally disabled. Literally, hundreds have been cared for in the homes of our leaders. Refugees, immigrant workers, the homeless, and those who have nowhere else to go, come to our community's leaders for the holidays. We have joked that one particular family is the newest mission in town.

In 3 John we are told "to give to those who have gone out for the Name." These evangelists are also in our homes, and as the Scripture mentions, some have entertained angels unaware. We hope that we are some of those people.

Homes of all Christians should be given to hospitality. All Christian homes should be open to those who need a place. As our kids leave home and see the church in America, they are finding that they often don't recognize the church and individual Christians in the larger American culture. It seems that they were cocooned by the danger of the inner city. The larger society may be physically safer than where they grew up, but they're not looking for safety. They're looking for Christians whose faith produces action, Christians who practice genuine hospitality.

KIND FRIENDS THE REWARD
FOR HELPING OTHERS

You have met older people who will tell you that they didn't know they were poor until someone told them. This is the case for our family. Even though our income falls under most of the government's measures for poverty, it turns out that we are the richest poor people you can imagine.

We have known lack on many levels. There are times when we think that we can't stand the gravity of the condition any more. God has comforted us and has granted us the delights of the intangible—peace, answered prayers, forgiveness, hope and the warm assurance that the Creator listens to our prayers. We have it all, and more. Except cash.

Isaiah 58 tells us that God will hear those who care for the needy and He will be their protector. We have believed God would raise up a church among the poor and bless it. That blessing has spilled over to our family. First of all we have always been too poor for child care. So our children are usually with us. They see ministry as part of the work they were born into. We often say we do ministry like people ran the family farm a generation ago. Everyone has a part to play. Our children, some now young adults, are part of ministry with us. Others of them are starting their own ministries. It's just what they do and we are pleased. Their ministry-minded grandparents are pleased, too.

Our inner city home, a converted duplex, has eight bedrooms. It has been home for both the church and our extended family. Jim's mother and grandmother lived with us while the church was meeting in our house. Since those days our house has been home to interns, friends, and occasionally bands that stopped by for the night.

We have a table that easily seats twenty. During one Vacation Bible School we had eighty children on the stairs and in our dining room. We have worn out our house. But we are excited to have built lasting welcome with dear friends who have come around to help. These friends are from every walk of life including the homeless and nearly destitute, as well as doctors, lawyers, government officials, and PhDs. Our table is a place of warm food and delightful discussion.

When one of the families at church was in trouble with Child Protective Services, the church sprang into action. We cleaned. We worked. We counseled the family. We went to court. And in the end the two children we fostered were adopted into our family. We thought that we were caring for them; now after their adoption we see that God was caring for us. More children in the family! What richness, what an opportunity.

Adoption is part of the culture of our church. A few more children are added to our leadership families regularly. We, as a church, care for our biological children, our adopted children, our foster children, and many unattended children at our services.

In the last few years God added more foster children to our family. We are so thankful to care for these children. They are part of a family we have known for four generations. They are a joy and we are made even richer for having them. These two more were adopted this year.

We have never owned a new car and that has never bothered us. It's just not part of the budget and it doesn't seem to fit in our view of ministry. We like it when people have extra cars and are not sure what to do with their old vehicles. We didn't buy a car for a stretch of twenty years. It's not that we got a good one and it lasted. Oh, no! We have had dozens of cars. Friends have joked that somehow we have been involved with mercy killing of automobiles. We get them when they are old and put them out of their misery. Often, our cars are broken down somewhere. When we find ourselves walking, we pray and our friends rally to help. We were given a 1964 Rambler once. These cars run when they want, but when they are running they serve our family, church, and neighborhood. Our cars can tell you this one thing about us: we have friends.

We find that many of our affluent friends offer us opportunities that are beyond our position in society. We have been offered collector quality cars to drive when we have been broken down. We have been asked to government events, country clubs, private dinner clubs, vacations, second homes, and group retreats. We love to travel and beauty is at the heart of what God has made.

The Lord tells us that He has given us all things to enjoy. Even though our friends are sincere in their generosity, we rarely go. Often we don't have the clothes, car, or available cash to make these opportunities work. On other occasions we know that our presence might demand a lot of explaining on our host's part. But our main concern is that if our impoverished friends don't fit into that world, then maybe we should wait until one day they can.

These ministry decisions have been hard choices. In every area that we look we can count the cost of sacrifice. Yet, we see that we have given nothing up that has not been replaced with something better.

We have been cash-strapped, but in the area of friends and family we have the lion's share of blessing. We recommend ministry with a poverty of cash. It seems to come with a great richness that includes God and His people!

31 IDEAS ON WHERE TO BEGIN

If you don't know where to begin and you want to, here's a list of things a group of poor people we know have already done. Maybe it will inspire you to do these things. Maybe you could do more.

Adopt a child, maybe a few.
Become a regular part of a widow's life.
Buy the same nice thing for a poor person that you would buy for yourself.
Sell something and give the money to a poor person.
Start letting a church use your home as a church plant location.
Keep a guest room better than your master bedroom.
Start a food pantry in your church.

Meet the cashier at the convenience store and find a way to get to know him.

Start a free clinic.

Start a free school.

Invite poor people to Thanksgiving at your house.

Clean the restroom at a place the poor gather.

Buy an extra house and charge below-market rent.

Plant an urban garden and give the produce away.

Take a poor kid shopping for school clothes.

Use your social capital to give a hand up to a needy person or family.

Give money to those who need a loan.

Buy street art.

Let your kids volunteer at a shelter or youth center.

Use your skills to better others for free.

Get your relationships to support a cause.

Start a camp for inner-city children.

Take a poor person on vacation with your family.

Open your home up when the shelters are full.

Make sure every stranded motorist gets home on your way home from work.

Get your foster care license.

Start a drug and alcohol recovery program.

Develop a job training class, such as a certified nurse's assistant class.

Provide tutorial assistance to kids of all ages.

Encourage everyone around you, especially if they are needy.

Provide regular meals where conversation can be had about meeting the needs of the poor.

THE TRANSGENDERS WE HAVE
KNOWN AND LOVED.

OK that title was just for shock. But not nearly as shocking as the stories that the church has because of our outreach. It also suggests that God does things beyond our imaginations.

Rebecca asked why we did not reach out to the prostitutes on 10th Street. She was not used to our church giving excuses why we couldn't do something. We are the church of "yes you can!" If Christ is in you, you can do all things through Him.

Jim explained that we have tried over the last 20 years to minister to many of the prostitutes on 10th Street. We feel like we have had little success. We've always been clear to preach the gospel to anyone we come in contact with. Someone hungry, or in need of clothing, finds that we are a warm, welcoming, and non-judgmental group. We often say of ourselves "we are just like one starving man telling another starving man where the food is." All of us need a savior. Yet some of us are so far into the consequences of sin that if we don't come out soon, we will find death right around the corner. That is the case for many of the prostitutes. Drugs and the promise of one more euphoria is what drive women to these near death experiences.

Rebecca did some research into who ministers to the prostitutes in our city. There are very few groups. This is an extremely difficult work. But before long we were steered to work with a group called Agape Alliance. They have a 12 step program and we are thankful that their outreach is housed in our church building. The thing that we had to get used to is that they also cared for men who identify as women.

A year ago we didn't know any transgenders. Today we know, and express the love of God to eleven. We only know a small percentage of those in the city, but we know the most desperate. These men, who identify as women, are in rebellion to their own DNA, but they, like the dozens of women prostitutes, need the Lord.

How were they ever going to hear about the Lord if we never welcomed them. "Blessed are the merciful. They shall receive mercy." We want mercy!

FAITHFULNESS UNTIL THE END

If there is any human key to Neighborhood Fellowship's success, it is the servant attitude, humility, and faithfulness of the leaders of the church. Although our family gets quite a bit of the attention, the truth is that there are six elders, all of whom have had formal training for ministry. These families also have faithfully worked out our relationships over the last twenty years. They are Phil and Linda Jackson (Linda is already with the Lord), Barry and Jessie Glaser, Mike and Cindy Hale, Doug and Joy Elliott, and Phil and Debra Jackson.

This group, and the other workers added to us, are first and foremost theologically driven. They act out our theology in practical and loving ways. Our one deacon, Aaron, and his wife Beth are terrific examples.

The Apostle Paul says, "Work out your own salvation for it is God in you who causes you to will and to do." This crowd understands their responsibility to work and hear from God. They have lovingly come to a community they have background with and they have identified with the urban poor here.

131

They see themselves in the same need of God as those they are reaching out to. They know that God is not waiting for them to come up with some good ideas for implementation. He has already planned out what they are to do. This faithful group is guided in those relationships by God's Word that calls us to honor and respect. The Scripture tells us to treat older men as fathers. There is honor for wisdom.

They also know how to pray. When we ask God for something, we know what we are asking for. Even now, any of our leaders can tell you what we expect the future to hold. We have a list of a couple of institutions that we have yet to start. Church is mission. We are on a mission so we pray and act like we are going somewhere and doing something. We are on a mission and the God who can do anything, abundantly more than we ask or think, is the ultimate authority in the universe. We start and finish with prayer to Him.

There are also faithful young people who have added their strength to the middle-aged visionaries who want to see God's will done on earth as it is in heaven. Faithfulness and a commitment to meet the needs of those in greatest need has been the hallmark of Neighborhood Fellowship. The leaders have found their purpose single-minded and their hearts inclusive. As a result, many have joined in to help from all walks of life. Many volunteers who joined with us have also been faithful. They have worked year after year to help move the church and vision forward.

We praise God for those who have given. We praise Him more for those who have worked, and even more for those who have prayed. God is good, and He has added those who minister with us. What a joyful thing it is to get up in the morning and not wonder if your life, work, prayers, or visions count for anything lasting or are in line with God's plan. Neighborhood Fellowship is a blessed community where people, friends, and co-workers can add their spiritual gifts to the deep relationships established and find purposeful place in ministry. We see that the ministry we are called to is something anyone can do. If we can do these things with God's help, then imagine what more the Lord might do with you.

QUESTIONS FOR REFLECTION:

How can you risk more for the Gospel?

How is politeness different from love?

How do you speak the truth in love? Give examples.

What do God's riches look like?

What more can you do for the Kingdom?

How is this verse working out in your life? "Work out your own salvation for it is God in you who causes you to will and to do."

Are you on mission? How do you know?

46042447R00091

Made in the USA
Middletown, DE
20 July 2017